What people are saying about

The Witch's Book of Simples

Since the rise of drug-resistant bacteria, and of viral pandemics, more and more people have been turning to the natural world for answers, and in particular to herbs. In her new book, Melusine Draco shows how using a single herb in a "Simple" can be used to treat a variety of ailments, including the ubiquitous virus.

She takes you through each step of the process from preparing to grow herbs, to planting and caring for them, through harvesting and using them. Each recipe contains a single herb along with other ingredients that can be used to treat whatever ails you. This is the most basic form of herbal medicine and has its roots back into prehistory. It is the art of the healer in its most simple way, traditionally practiced by the village midwives, traditional witches, the cunning folk, the pellars, and of course, the apothecaries.

The Witch's Book of Simples book is a fantastic resource, full of a wealth of herbal knowledge garnered over hundreds of years. This book is highly recommended to anyone starting out on their journey into herbs.

Tish Romanov The Old Apothecary

The Witch's Book of Simples

The Simple Arte of Domestic Folk Medicine

The Witch's Book of Simples

The Simple Arte of Domestic Folk Medicine

Mélusine Draco

MOON
BOOKS
Winchester, UK
Washington, USA

JOHN HUNT PUBLISHING

First published by Moon Books, 2022
Moon Books is an imprint of John Hunt Publishing Ltd., No. 3 East Street, Alresford
Hampshire SO24 9EE, UK
office@jhpbooks.net
www.johnhuntpublishing.com
www.moon-books.net

For distributor details and how to order please visit the 'Ordering' section on our website.

ISBN: 978 1 78904 789 9
978 1 78904 790 5 (ebook)
Library of Congress Control Number: 2021934899

A CIP catalogue record for this book is available from the British Library.

Design: Matthew Greenfield

UK: Printed and bound by CPI Group (UK) Ltd, Croydon, CR0 4YY
Printed in North America by CPI GPS partners

We operate a distinctive and ethical publishing philosophy in
all areas of our business, from our global network of authors to
production and worldwide distribution.

Contents

Keep it Simple

A Simple is a philtre derived from a single herb and was an important element among the natural resources of the parish-pump witch, wise-women and cunning-folk. Simples are common kitchen 'stuff' that has been handed down through generations of country people in the form of family cures for everyday ailments. Or as William Fernie wrote in his *Herbal Simples* (1897)

> *The art of Simpling is as old with us as our British hills. It aims at curing common ailments with simple remedies culled from the soil, or got from home resources near at hand.*

These were no fancy recipes with magical formulae, and, often given as a tisane, the women of the household were able to use the remedies to treat common ailments suffered by her family. And, this elementary form of domestic plant medicine can be as simple as a cup of chamomile tea made from flowers picked fresh from our own garden to aid sleep. This was the most elementary way to use medicinal plants since no fancy recipes or scientific acumen was needed as Simples were often given as an infusion or used as a poultice or compress. But this element of traditional witchcraft has long been in the shadows ...

Author's Note

As most of my readers will know, I have a fascination for odd and obscure historical facts that are hidden away in the millions of sources that outstrip and confound the confines of the Internet – it's finding them that presents the stimulation and the challenge. Because if we merely rely on the regurgitated information of contemporary paganism not only does our mind become stagnant, but for those who follow the Craft of the witch, so do our magical abilities.

Over the years I have also incorporated a great deal of folk-cunning and country-lore into my books on witchcraft with a view to preserving that knowledge for future generations. Much of what even those of my grandparents' generation once knew is now lost because it was never recorded for posterity. True, there are numerous pagan books written about similar subjects but it is obvious that a large number of writers don't have the countryside in their blood and fail to reflect the magic and mystery of growing up in an uncomplicated rural environment. Strangely enough, these sentiments are often now viewed as some form of *elitism* but I prefer to go back to the roots of learning rather than consult something that has been cobbled together from different popular titles without any true grounding in Nature.

Finally, special thanks must go to medical herbalist Tish Romanov of The Old Apothecary for giving *The Witch's Book of Simples* the once over to make sure I wasn't about to kill anyone, or that my brain hadn't failed during the long years since I was first introduced to (and used) these simple domestic plant remedies ... and for adding the warnings, cautions and dangers where applicable. **Mélusine Draco**

Web: www.covenofthescales.com and www.templeofkhem.com

Blog: https://wordpress.com/view/melusine-draco.blog

Blog: https://theoldapothecary.wordpress.com/

Disclaimer

Natural medicines have been an integral ingredient of traditional witchcraft for centuries and the information contained within the text of *The Witch's Book of Simples - the simple arte of domestic folk medicine* is compiled for interest and information only. Neither the author nor the publisher is responsible for the inappropriate, unprofessional, criminal or ill-fated misuse of such plants. Let the wise reader learn and the fool beware.

Go ... learn things.

Introduction

Keep it Simple

A 'Simple' is a philtre derived from a single herb and was an important element among the natural resources of the parish-pump witch, wise-women and cunning-folk's healing remedies. Simples are common kitchen 'stuff' that has been handed down through generations of country people in the form of family cures for everyday ailments, despite that by the 11-12th-centuries in Europe, most of the old pagan practices were all but replaced by Christian variants. Old festivals had been assimilated and turned into saints' days. And the 'cunning-folk' now called on Jesus, Mary and the saints in their herbal folk charms.

Occasionally, however, pagan elements did remain unrecognised, and therefore remained unmolested. In *Mastering Herbalism*, Paul Huson quotes an example of an impressive spell used by 12th-century herbalists and translated from *Early English Magic and Medicine* by Charles Singer [taken from the proceedings of the British Academy, vol. iv]

Here the earth is invoked as a mother in time-honoured fashion. She is even addressed as 'goddess', which is extraordinary considering the growing climate of suspicion and persecution of heresy ...

Or William Coles in his *Nature's Paradise*, or, *Art of Simpling* (1657) being of the opinion

that if those of these times would but be ... as industrious to search into the secrets of the nature of Herbs, as some of former times, and make a tryll of them as they did, [they] should no doubt find the force of Simples ... no less Effectual, than that of Compounds, to which this present ago is too much addicted. Thus I have broken the

Nut of Herbarisme, do thou take out the Kernel and eat it and much good may it do thee.

Or as William Fernie later wrote in his *Herbal Simples* (1897)

The art of Simpling is as old with us as our British hills. It aims at curing common ailments with simple remedies culled from the soil, or got from home resources near at hand. Since the days of the Anglo-Saxons such remedies have been chiefly herbal; insomuch that the word 'drug' came originally from their verb drigan, to dry, as applied to medicinal plants.

Simples - from the Latin *Singula plica* - meaning 'a single purpose' - at that time, signified medicines made from a single herb, while those made from several different plants were known as 'compounds'. These were no fancy recipes with magical formulae, and, often given as an infusion or tisane, the woman of the household being able to use these remedies to treat common ailments suffered by her family. And this elementary form of healing can be as simple as a cup of chamomile tea made from flowers picked fresh from our own garden to aid sleep.

'Medicine is mine; what herbs and Simples grow/In fields and forests, all their powers I know,' wrote Dryden and this sentiment is reflected in the fact that the olde herbals give a glimpse of a way of life in other generations, that is *not* always suggestive or recommended we try for ourselves. Herbalist, Nicholas Culpeper, whose name is still a household word with any who have an interest in natural medicine, and who published in 1652 for the ...

benefit of the Commonwealth, his Compleat Method whereby a man may cure himself of being sick, for three-pence charge, with such things only as grow in England, they being most fit for English bodies'.

It would, however, be inadvisable to follow his advice today because:

It has not been thought expedient to include among the Simples for homely uses of cure such powerfully poisonous plants as Monkshood (Aconite), Deadly Nightshade (Belladonna), Foxglove (Digitalis), Hemlock or Henbane (except for some outward uses), and the like dangerous herbs, these being beyond the province of domestic medicine, whilst only to be administered under the advice and guidance of a qualified prescriber. [Herbal Simples, 1897]

Those of us who grew up with these various herbal remedies plucked straight from the garden or hedgerow had no idea that within our own lifetime, this first-hand knowledge would disappear forever. For example: that the daisy-like flowers of chamomile have long been used in burns remedies by making a compress using a cotton cloth soaked in a strong infusion of chamomile ... or, alternatively, diluted and distilled witch hazel that can be bought in small bottles from the chemist to treat those irritating household burns from the iron and hot oil splatters. For sunburn a linen compress of cold milk was perhaps the best way to sooth the burned area. Or a teaspoon of salt dissolved in a glass of warm water to temporarily soothe a sore throat by gargling; or an infusion of fresh, sliced ginger to relieve nausea; slices of cucumber or cold teabags for sore and puffy eyes ... and, of course, prunes for constipation. While there were all sorts of remedies for insect bites ... from lavender, basil, lemon/ lime or apple cider vinegar.

Medicinal herbs have been grown in gardens since they were recorded in Egyptian frescoes and the descriptions of the Roman *Hortus,* but it was the monastery gardens of the early Christian era, following the collapse of the Roman Empire, that began the Western tradition of herb growing and herbalism. This concept formed the basis for the popular novels and television series, *The*

Cadfael Chronicles and the thought-provoking spin-off - *Brother Cadfael's Herb Garden* - an illustrated companion to medieval plants and their uses – which chronicles the plants that would have been known to witches of the day.

As magic and religion, biology and medicine, botany and philosophy all originally coexisted side by side (rather than being separate and distinct sciences), elaborate rituals grew up around the gathering and use of plants and herbs. To be most efficacious they had to be picked and prepared at specific times of the day or year ... Some of these 'magical' plants venerated by pagans were later Christianised by a simple name change. Although references to herbs, including spells and prescriptions, have been preserved from the civilizations of ancient Egypt, Mesopotamia, India and China, it was the classical works of the Greeks and Romans that dominated European science and medicine up to and throughout the medieval period.

The story of herbal healing has an impressive history, and in her highly readable book, *The Healing Power of Celtic Plants*, Dr Angela Paine traces the remarkable story of the Physicians of Myddfai. The knowledge of medicine in Wales goes back to ancient Celtic times when it was handed down orally through many generations and reveals that the Welsh physicians possessed knowledge of Greek, Roman and Arabic healing plant lore. During the 13th-century, a Prince of South Wales, Rhys Gryg, instructed his court physician, Rhiwallon, to gather together the knowledge of medicinal plants and their methods of application and to write it down in Welsh. This would enable others to make use of the information both then and during the centuries that followed.

Rhiwallon lived at Myddfai, and the countryside around the village is still very rich in medicinal plants. They include *Valeriana officinalis, Filipendula ulmaria, Scrophularia nodosa, Digitalis purpurea, Plantago spp.,* and *Achiltea millefolium*; the uses to which the Myddfai Physicians put these plants, and others, are described in their writings. 'Magical' plants such as *Verbena officinalis* and *Viscum album*, which have Druidic connections are also included and some of these are still used today by herbalists, with many of the prescriptions of the Physicians remaining as relevant today as they were in the distant past.

Although the Anglo-Saxons were interested in herbs, the main research and development in herbal medicine after the collapse of the Roman Empire was carried out by Arab physicians, who based much of their learning on the writings of the ancient Greeks. After the Norman conquest of England in 1066, many Anglo-Saxon manuscripts were destroyed and replaced with books written exclusively in Latin. Although the Romans introduced many plants into Britain, it was the Emperor Charlemagne who actively encouraged the spread of herbs and spices throughout Europe; decreeing that each city within his empire should have a garden planted with '*all herbs*'. The foreign emperor's edicts, however, did not reach as far as Britain and during the Dark Ages it was left to the monasteries to preserve and augment the legacy of herbal knowledge abandoned after the fall of Rome. Fortunately for posterity, at the Dissolution of the Monasteries c.1536, some valuable books and manuscripts on the subject found their way into private libraries.

Dr Richard Aspin searched through 17th-century recipe books to find out more about the herbal medicine found in Shakespeare's plays because locally harvested wild herbs were the foundation of medical practice in England of the time. Some plants were cultivated in kitchen and herb gardens, but they differed little from their wild equivalents. Exotic herbs – that is, plants from overseas – were beginning to play an increasing role in the English pharmacopoeia, but whether native or exotic, 'Simples' – 'those medicinal substances that nature provided without any human intervention' – still formed the basis of Elizabethan domestic medicine.

In Shakespeare's time there was a London street, named Bucklersbury (near today's Mansion House), so noted for the number of apothecaries who sold Simples and sweet-smelling herbs that in *The Merry Wives of Windsor*, Sir John Falstaff describes the dandified fops of his day as *'Lisping hawthorn buds that smell like Bucklersbury in simple time.'*

William Fernie also made rare mention of the 'green men' [and women] who were first licensed in the Elizabethan Wild Herb Act to gather herbs and roots from wild, uncultivated land – but it was an occupation that had been going strong since the late 14th-century. A new kind of medical herbalist had evolved – the apothecary – who purchased plants collected from the countryside by these wandering herb collectors. In *Green Pharmacy*, Barbara Griggs records that, during the 17th-century, herbs could also be bought direct from the herb women in Newgate Market or Covent Garden. According to Fernie:

> *Coming down to the first part of the present [19th] century, we find purveyors of medicinal and savory herbs then wandered over the whole of England in quest of useful Simples as were in constant demand at most houses for the medicine-chest, the store-closet, or the toilet-table. These rustic practitioners of the healing art were known as 'green men', who carried with them their portable apparatus for distilling essences, and for preparing their herbal extracts. In token of their giving formally officiated in this capacity, there may yet be seen in London and elsewhere about the country, taverns bearing the curious sign of The Green Man & [his] Still*

The Green Man & Still was a tavern originally situated at 335 Oxford Street, London and was also a coaching inn (a 1792 map shows it at the entrance to a stagecoach yard), the starting point/ terminus of several stage coach routes out of London. Although the original tavern closed and re-located, it retained the *Green Man & Still* name as late as the early 1920s. Another *Green Man*

& Still is recorded at 161 Whitecross Street, Clerkenwell in 1789 run by one Peter Richardson/ victualler from Sun Fire Office records held at the London Metropolitan Archives. It closed in 2006 and remained empty until it became a coffee shop in 2011. The 'Green Man' became a popular name for English pubs in the 17th-century (when the Distiller's Company *Green Man & Still* heraldic arms were still in common use), although most inn signs tend to feature the familiar foliated face of church architecture; while the 'green men' of Elizabethan times probably merged into the cunning-folk tradition and faded into oblivion.

The confusion between the two grew from a simple misunderstanding. Julia Somerset (Lady Raglan) only published one article on folklore in her lifetime, which appeared in the journal *Folklore* - formerly *The Folk-Lore Journal* (1883–1889) and *The Folk-Lore Record* (1878–1882) - and it almost certainly had a more lasting influence than anything written by her folklorist husband. She claimed to have investigated the supposed mythic-ritualistic origins underlying popular cultural motifs, but her focus of study was the foliate head seen everywhere in European medieval church decoration of the eleventh to sixteenth centuries. Before Lady Raglan's intervention, this figure had been anonymous. She gave him a name: the Green Man.

The Green Man largely disappeared during the neo-Classical period and Industrial Revolution of the eighteenth and nineteenth centuries, although this time also saw the rise in popularity of the related figure of Jack-in-the-Green at May Day festivities (and rather mysteriously having a particular association with chimney sweeps in the early years). Leaf-covered Green or Wild Men had been appearing in town pageants for centuries, possibly as live representations of the Green Man of church architecture, but the first attested appearance of Jack-in-the-Green was as recent as 1775. Indeed, one might have expected the Green Man to disappear completely in this age of science and rationality, and for a time he seemed to have done just that. But he has never entirely faded away.

In *Memory, Wisdom & Healing; The History of Domestic Plant Medicine*, Gabrielle Hatfield has gathered together material from manuscripts, letters, diaries and personal interviews to produce a detailed picture of the use of domestic remedies in Britain from 1700 to the 21st-century. And although historians have neglected this captivating subject, her extensive research caused her to make an extremely important observation:

> *How far have we misinterpreted the role of the 'cunning man' or 'wise woman' of the past? Perhaps many of them were the equivalent of this informant's aunt: well versed in plant medicines, and therefore able to help family and friends in time of sickness; just this and no more: there may have been no ritual or magic in their home medicines. This is not to deny the existence of magical and ritualistic practices in medicine. To deny this would be to fly in the face of evidence. What I am suggesting is that family plant-medicine was relatively free of these elements. Indeed, the use of native plants in self-help medicine in this country may have been the one constant thread in the history of medical practice. Magical and religious and astrological practices associated with physic waxed and waned in popularity, but the use of 'simples' remained constant: a standby for country people in times of illness.*

Knowledge was handed down orally and only rarely were written records kept for posterity in rural communities. And, as Gabrielle Hatfield also observes, what few records there are on the subject have usually been written by those with no direct experience of country remedies.

> *Such writing tends to treat fragments of information as curios, of a rather quaint nature, to be collected together like a collection of dried butterflies. This not only removes the information from its context, it also tends to lead to a condescending attitude towards*

the users of such remedies. The very word 'folk' has come to have a patronizing ring to it, and too often accounts of folk medicine concentrate on the bizarre and fanciful. Taken out of context, and sometimes even quoted quite wrongly, this has built up a picture of folk medicine as a collection of odd and anachronistic rituals, practiced by the ignorant and superstitious. In reality, domestic [plant] medicine was a necessary tool for survival ... and it is our loss if we dismiss this wisdom too lightly.

Up until the 18th-century, botany and medicine were closely allied but they subsequently drew apart and developed as separate disciplines. This is not to say that the old herbal remedies disappeared: traditions were kept alive in many rural locations, and in some countries, they never fell from use. In Europe the day-to-day use of herbs remained more widely practiced than it did in Britain. Mrs. Maud Grieve, whose famous herbal was published in 1931, did much to promote the renewed interest in herbs in Britain in the 20th century.

What we *do* know is that a preparation made with fresh ingredients is many times more effective than one made from dried plants. And while dominant flavour compounds in some *herbs* thrive when *dried,* the *fresh* version of more delicate *herbs* always provide more flavor than dried ones. Opinions often vary, but in general, we need to use three times the amount of fresh herbs as dried ... so if a recipe calls for one tablespoon of dried basil from a jar, use three tablespoons of *fresh* basil. Or 1 unit of dried herb equals 3 units of fresh.

When beginning to explore the world of domestic plant medicine, traditional herbalism holds that it is best to start with them one at a time to fully experience the taste, the essence, and the benefit of a single plant. Try experimenting with the herbs, keeping a note of the effect they have (or don't have), since not everyone reacts to particular herbs in quite the same way. There are some herbs that are recommended to be taken regularly even when we're not ill, such as those that are rich in iron and vitamins added to salads.

Simpler, Susan Weed, believes that using one herb at a time gives us unparalleled opportunities to observe and make use of the subtle differences that are at the very heart of herbal medicine.

When we use Simples we are more likely to notice the many variables that affect each herb: including where it grows, the year's weather, how we harvest it, our preparation, and the dosage. The many variables within one plant ensures that our Simple remedy nonetheless touches many aspects of a person and heals deeply.

By growing our own plants from seed, or buying small plants from a garden centre means that we know *exactly* what we are using but it isn't enough, however, to *read* that rosemary can be used as a lotion applied to wounds, or that tea made with dried thyme cures a hangover. To get the most out of Nature's medicine chest, we need to be familiar with the plants themselves and get used to handling them ... but it is not *always* advisable to utilise Nature's local bounty. There may be plants in profusion on urban waste ground and open verges but all may be coated with industrial and vehicle emissions, dust, grime ... not to mention the gallons of urine emptied over them daily by a procession of passing dogs!

Also resist the popular alternative - to stock up with the entire range from your local health shop – and instead start with one multi-purpose *fresh* herb at a time. Experiment and get a feel for each individual plant and all its uses, so that the interaction comes naturally. Begin with those commonly in domestic use: such as the familiar herbs listed in the traditional folk song, *Scarborough Fair* – *'parsley, sage, rosemary and thyme'* - since all can be obtained ready-grown in pots from a local supermarket.

Be warned, however, that supermarket bought herbs have

often been force-grown and rarely survive very long in a warm kitchen, never mind being transplanted outside. Another reason is that *supermarket herbs* are actually many plants all squashed together in one pot and because the plants are so tightly packed, each one tries to grow up to the light, producing leggy plants without many side shoots. All of this means that they will droop sooner or later and give up the ghost, so keep them on a sunny windowsill and enjoy them in the kitchen until you can replace them with your own hardier home-grown plants.

And this is our first lesson in Simpling ... sitting in a comfortable chair, we hold the crushed herb in a tissue or handkerchief up to our nostrils and breathe in the scent of the plant. Fresh herbs are best for this task, although dried ones can be used if we have none growing in our garden, or in pots on our window sill. We allow the scent to carry us away into another world and see what images or memories come through in this semi-drowsy or relaxed state. We try each one of the herbs in turn over several days and see which has the strongest effect on our senses. All of these plants are normal culinary herbs and have no hallucinogenic qualities but they do have the power to trigger the imagination ... and memories. Try it and see for yourself.

Endpiece: Simples are used as quick, house-hold remedies in domestic folk-medicine and not intended for long-term treatments. If symptoms persist, a pharmacist, doctor or professional herbalist should be consulted because self-diagnosis and prescription can lead to problems. Adverse reactions to plant remedies *can* happen – even though many an amateur will claim that because plants are natural, they can't harm! – and the *Yoga Journal* posted an interesting piece on the subject:

> *If for relief you turn to medicinal herbs, many of which come from the same plant families as the allergens; in looking for the cure for your allergies, are you just adding to the problem? People can have*

an allergic reaction to anything and although rare, medicinal herbs are no exception. We should also bear in mind that overdoing it with herbs can also have ill effects, so take only the recommended dosage and if we develop any signs - rashes, hives, itching - we should stop taking the herb. Some herbal products have been found to be contaminated by pesticides and heavy metals, so select only reputable brands if using shop-bought preparations.

Everyday kitchen cupboard ingredients can also be used for curing little ailments and back in the day, these were automatically administered whenever the need arose. Over-the-counter remedies still cost a fortune and were often no more effective than those old-fashioned cures our grandmothers handed out. Although the witch or wise woman's modern kitchens might not have those old, evocative smells of yesteryear, the contents of the kitchen cupboard and larder (if you're lucky enough to have one) should still contain these precious ingredients.

For example: 'bicarb' or baking soda has dozens of uses for minor medical complaints and personal health issues if you run out of a normal healthcare product. Create a breath freshener by adding one teaspoon in half a glass of water, swish, spit and rinse: odours are neutralized, not just covered up. It also serves as an emergency toothpaste. Use as a facial scrub by making a paste of three parts baking soda to one part water. This is gentle enough for daily use: rub in a gentle circular motion to exfoliate the skin and rinse clean. Pat baking soda onto your underarms to neutralise body odour and sprinkle in shoes to freshen.

'Bicarb' is a safe and effective antacid to relieve heartburn, sour stomach and/or acid indigestion. It is also standby for anyone suffering from cystitis or urinary tract infection. Take half a teaspoon in an 8fl oz glass of water a few times a day at the first sign of discomfort. For insect bites and bee stings make a paste out of baking soda and water, and apply as a salve onto affected skin. And to make a bath soak or refreshing foot bath, add 21oz of baking soda to the bath to neutralize acids on the skin and help wash away oil and perspiration; it also makes the skin feel very soft. A few tablespoons into the bathwater also helps relieve heat rash, hives, nappy rash and even haemorrhoids – a paste eases chicken pox itching, too. Soothe tired and aching feet by dissolving three tablespoons of baking soda in a bowl of warm water and soak feet. Gently scrub.

Chapter One

The Herb Garden

Anyone with a garden or a sunny windowsill can grow herbs because they are generally self-sufficient plants and, given a little care and attention, will thrive almost anywhere. Another advantage is that it doesn't take much space to create a herb garden, and even a selection of herbs grown in a window box will provide a small annual harvest. Having our own herb garden also gives us the opportunity to use herbs immediately after harvesting, which can be important when making Simples at home. Many herbs are grown for their beauty as well as their magical, medicinal and culinary uses – and have been an attractive feature in ornamental gardens for centuries.

Herbs freshly gathered are preferable to commercially prepared ones and although the healing properties of shop-bought herbs remain intact, their aromatic qualities are often depleted due to over-long storage. Nothing can compete with the home-grown plants. Most herbs that we might grow in a Simples garden will be mild and safe, such as mint or chamomile; others are common culinary herbs, like parsley, sage, rosemary, and thyme. For many of us, the decorative value is probably the most important thing, but the addition of knowing *how* to use our herbs for good health is a boon we can enjoy, too.

Beware, however, that some medicinal herbs are downright poisonous, especially if ingested without expert advice; foxglove, or digitalis, and lily-of-the-valley are two of those plants that are found in most cottage gardens. And even common, non-toxic herbs can have an adverse reaction on some of us because overdoing it with herbs *can* have ill effects, so take only the recommended dosages. *'People can have an allergic reaction to anything,'* says Mindy Green, director of education at the Herb

Research Foundation, 'and, although rare, medicinal herbs are no exception.'

When trying something new for the first time, eat only a very small amount to make sure there are no adverse effects, warns John Rensten of Forage London:

We are all wired differently and can respond differently too, so doing a simple tolerance test is a good habit to get into. By way of example, the root of common valerian is used to make a wonderful sedative tincture, rather like a natural valium, however in about ten percent of people it has the polar opposite effect and acts as a stimulant.

The family of herbs that most often causes reactions - the *Asteraceae,* or daisy family - includes ragweed, a common allergen, and healing herbs chamomile and echinacea. But does this mean that if we're allergic to ragweed, we'll automatically be allergic to its medicinal relatives as well? *'There is not a direct relationship,'* says Dr. Varro Tyler, author of *Tyler's Honest Herbal* and Professor Emeritus at Purdue University. *'But it does mean that you'll want to monitor your reactions more carefully when you take the herb.'* According to Dr Tyler, most allergic reactions produced by herbs are fairly mild - a runny nose, itchy skin or eyes, rashes, or hives but they don't appear to be very common.

So, let's get the warnings out of the way for a while ... accept that by and large, herbs *are* good for us, providing we don't take more than is beneficial for our health ... and get down to the important nitty-gritty about growing our own ...

The main requirement for cultivating herbs, of course, is growing them in the proper location. Most prefer full sun as long as regular summer temperatures aren't scorchers but if we have *very* hot summers, then we can consider planting in an area that gets morning sun and afternoon shade in the summertime, or a place that receives filtered light (such as under a tree that allows dappled light to pass through). Check the area several times during the day to make sure that it receives at least four hours of sunshine. Herbs are much easier to grow than many houseplants because all they need is a sunny, warm place and containers large enough for the plants to grow - and a convenient water supply. Sunny decks, patios, and other such areas are great for container gardening and by growing herbs in containers, we save ourselves the difficulty of digging that a garden plot requires.

Herb gardens can be as large or small as space permits from a window-sill to an elaborate Tudor knot, or a landscaped cartwheel design, but most of us make do with informal beds and borders. For the more ambitious there are themed gardens – especially those for Simple growing and commonly referred to as a physic or apothecary's garden that were the source of raw materials to heal the sick. In the tradition of monasteries, a range of Simples, or medicinal plants were grown in their own little plots. The advantage of keeping each herb in a separate bed was to make identification easier when it came to picking, as well as being an efficient method of cultivation on a small scale. It also provided easy access for planting, weeding and watering.

A modern garden of herbs for making simple home remedies draws on the best of these old traditions having an understated charm and being a low maintenance way to grow herbs. One idea is brought up to date by setting the plants among paving slabs at irregular intervals; another is a collection of wide-necked terracotta pots sunk into gravel in a simple configuration that is both functional and eye-catching. Or those themed gardens that echo the layout of the medieval monastery garden; an informal French-style *potager* or a more formal design of the symmetrical pathways and beds outlined with clipped box hedges and the apothecary or 'physic' garden.

If we want to pick herbs though out the year, all-weather paths or stepping stones should be incorporated into the design, and for convenience sake we don't want to locate the bed too far from the kitchen door. Another aspect to consider is also creating a place to relax – a small seating area surrounded by fragrant herbs because a herb garden offers multi-sensory pleasures. Whether we grow edible herbs or herbs for other uses, many of them have a bonus of fragrance and often the scent comes from their foliage that is intensified when they are crushed or broken ... so planting fragrant herbs where we will brush up against them when we walk by, is an easy way of enjoying a scented garden.

Gardening is a great stress-reliever but then, so is taking five minutes to sit out in a fragrant corner with a cup of tea and doing absolutely nothing in order to recharge our batteries. Although difficult to define, stress can be anything that disturbs a person's sense of well-being and just getting out in the sunshine can actually improve our mood because sunlight also provides an influx of vitamin D, and the fresh air that that goes with it is good for our health. Getting outdoors to work with our garden is a great excuse to get more of this good stuff while having our very own piece of nature right outside the back door can help us feel this connection. One of the most relaxing activities must surely be sitting in a quiet and cozy corner with a good book and so, we might just want to create such a nice spot in our backyard or garden for that purpose.

There's no better way to unwind at the end of a long, hard day than relaxing in a beautiful, tranquil garden area, no matter how small ... so, we create that outdoor space to be a feast for the senses and allow it to work its healing magic on eyes and nose, ears and fingertips by including tactile and strokable plants in our herb bed; while the drone of a big lazy bumblebee flying from flower to flower must be one of the most relaxing sounds on the planet. It's easy to forget the importance of touch, but running our fingers through soft, fluffy seed-heads can be just as therapeutic as stroking a pet. Grasses offer the full sensory spectrum and can be grouped together in colourful galvanized planters to add texture and variety throughout the year, while at the same time containing enthusiastic root-systems.

For the beds, choose aromatic leaves and scented flowers for a daily dose of accessible, stress-busting aromatherapy. We can create for ourselves a scented bower with roses, honeysuckle, or the beautiful evergreen star jasmine. Plant lavender, rosemary, thymes and tiny creeping mints; feverfew is a natural remedy for headaches, while sage is said to slow the ageing process. If we're too busy to enjoy them during the day, we can go for plants with a strong evening perfume such as honeysuckle, evening primrose, night-scented stocks or even tobacco that smells sweetest after dusk.

In general, and where possible choose a spot that receives six or more hours of sun, except in the very warmest regions, where herbs appreciate afternoon shade. Many herbs, like parsley, mint, and thyme, will actually grow just fine in partial shade. Growing herbs in pots in a patio area also allows us to shift the garden to the sun and are ideal where there may not be enough soil for a traditional in-ground garden. Pots of herbs offer more than just flavor. Many release fragrances as plants bask in the sun or you brush by leaves, and they look beautiful on any patio, deck, or even a tiered doorstep. Invasive herbs such as mint, sward, comfrey and tarragon are better grown in containers.

Planting herbs in containers is also a practical and ornamental way of displaying your favourites, particularly if garden space is limited. They can be positioned ready to hand for harvesting and will look completely different from year to year if replanted with a different selection of herbs. A window box is a good way to grow culinary herbs, providing access to a supply of fresh leaves and a sheltered site for the plants; replant the window box when the plants become crowded. An old stone sink is the perfect container for different varieties of thyme and a sprinkling of gardener's gravel between the plants turns it into an ornamental feature.

A pocketed herb-planter – known as a strawberry pot

from its original use – also makes an interesting display and enables a number of herbs to be grown in a small place though the relatively small amount of soil means it soon becomes overcrowded and dries out. A grouping of herbs in a variety of pots placed at different heights makes an attractive display on a flight of steps. Or a collection of herbs grouped in pots and using an old wooden barrow to display them gives extra height and adds visual interest in a small space. A mix of open ground planting and small containers at varying levels also creates an unusual focal point.

Herbs are traditionally associated with small gardens and raised beds. Thymes, sages and rosemary can form the shrubby framework among which more tender herbs, such as basil, can be grown in summer. Plant chives as an edging in rich, moist soil where they will get the sun, or fennel that is attractive in both its green and bronze feathery forms. The sages are also ornamental: there are purple, yellow, variegated and narrow-leaved grey forms. Not to mention orach that comes in reds, pinks and purples - depending on the variety; use golden marjoram; blue rue and flowering thymes to add lots of colour. The beds can be enclosed by dwarf hedges of lavender and yellow-button santolina; or chives and small dianthus; or let them all flow together with some tall alliums, swaying blue flax and colourful flashes of marigolds and nasturtiums. [RHA Really Small Gardens]

Edible herbs often have edible flowers. With many herbs - such as basil, mint, and stevia - leaf flavour begins to change (usually for the worse) once those flowers begin to form, so remove blossoms as soon as you see them. Other herbs, like chives and pineapple sage, flower throughout the growing season and make wonderful salad toppers.

Not all 'herbs' are cultivated, however, and many listed in the old herbals can still be found growing in the wild. In the most generally accepted sense, herbs are plants valued for their medicinal or aromatic qualities, and often grown and harvested for their unique properties. Many more can be found growing in, or under hedgerows, such as hawthorn and jack-by-the-hedge; on waysides and waste-ground like coltsfoot and plantain; and in woodlands we can find brambles and the wild garlic-tasting plant, ramsons.

The 'wild' is, of course, all part of the witch's herb garden since foraging is part and parcel of country living and utilising the healing properties of plants is an integral ingredient of traditional witchcraft and cunning-lore. It is, nevertheless, essential to know *exactly* what it is we are gathering because while garden herbs are easily identified, plants collected from the wild are usually less familiar and many are highly poisonous, even in the most unexpected of cases. For example:

It is widely known that the common field Buttercup, when pulled from the ground and carried in the palm of the hand, will redden and inflame the skin by the acrimony of its juices; or, if the bruised leaves are applied to any part they will excite a blistering of the outer cuticle, with a discharge of watery fluid from numerous small vesicles, while the tissues beneath become red, hot and swollen ... a medical tincture of the Buttercup , if taken in small doses, and applied, will promptly and effectively cure the same troublesome ailment ... [Herbal Simples, 1897]

This is the same flower that children picked in the meadows and held up to their playmate's chin to see if they liked butter. But the real reason the flowers seem to shine with an intense glittering yellow is nothing to do with butter but about advertising the plants to insect pollinators from a great distance. And beggars used poultices of crushed buttercup leaves to inflict their own skin with harmful ulcers. The purpose of this seemingly ridiculous form of self-mutilation was to arouse pity and possibly a few pennies. As a result, the plant was rurally called Lazarus, or beggar's weed.

Similarly, the *Apiaceae*, or plants of the parsley or carrot family (previously known as *Umbelliferae*) includes some wonderful edible plants like the carrot and parsnip, plus more aromatic varieties found in our spice cabinets, such as anise, celery, chervil, coriander, caraway, cumin, dill, fennel and of course, parsley. But unlike the mustard or mint families, the parsleys are not all safe for picking and eating. In fact, the parsley family is among the most important plant species to learn, since it includes the deadliest plants in the world: poison hemlock and water hemlock. And giant hogweed, whose sap, when combined with moisture and sunlight can burn the skin and eyes; potentially resulting in painful blistering, long-time sun sensitivity, permanent scarring, and even lasting blindness!

By contrast, the elder tree has long been associated with witchcraft, folklore and religion, which may partly reflect the wide range of medicinal uses of many parts of the plant because its country name is '*poor man's medicine chest*'. Traditional winter cold remedies using elder include elderberry wine and elder flowers combined in a hot infusion with peppermint and yarrow. Elder leaves make a useful ointment for bruises, sprains and wounds. An ointment made from elder flowers is excellent for chilblains and stimulating local circulation. The flowers make popular hay fever treatments and their diuretic effect can also help to reduce congestion.

We also need to be mindful about the location where we find our wild herbs. Much has been written about the damage to human health from nitrogen oxides given off by traffic emissions, but the damage to sensitive plants has gone largely unnoticed. Excessive nitrogen also comes from ammonia in fertilisers and manures, with much of the countryside awash with nitrates running off farmland. More than a third of Britain's wild flowering plants need low levels of nutrients in the soil, and they are suffering from too much nitrogen raining down from the atmosphere. That onslaught is having a devastating effect on 90% of sensitive plant habitats in England and Wales, such as woodlands, grasslands, heaths and bogs, according to the charity Plantlife. And in some wild areas, nitrogen-guzzling plants such as nettles have run riot and swamped the natural wild plants.

Whether urban foraging or in the countryside, we should wash anything we find at ground level. Dogs' wee, due to clever canine leg cocking may be on plants a good bit higher so I never eat anything as I go along unless I'm sure it's out of the dog wee zone (how high can an Irish wolf hound or Great Dane pee anyway?), or unless it's in an area I'm sure no dogs could access. Avoid plants that look scorched or blackening, this could be either as a result of animal urine or far worse, the use of chemical pesticides. Just use your common sense and select plants, fruits, nuts and other foods in the same way you'd do in a shop, leaving behind anything that isn't in great condition. Lastly, and to overstate the obvious, don't pick anything from the base of city trees however healthy it looks (wee is a great source of nitrogen and plants thrive on it). [Forage London]

By today's definition, a herb can be any plant with leaves, seeds, or flowers used for flavouring, food, medicine, or perfume but perhaps we are safer sticking to the common or garden herbs we all know and love because most herbs that we might grow in a Simples garden will be mild and safe, such as mint or chamomile. While parsley is a popular folk remedy for bad breath and chives may offer a number of health benefits, including prevention of cancer and mood enhancement.

A garden of Simples, composed of a selection of medicinal herbs, have been in use at least since the Middle Ages, though plants have been grown for medical purposes long before that. Even the smallest herb garden will bestow well-being, in addition to the pleasure gained from taking care of it. To admire our own home-grown herbs and harvest them in the preparation of making some beneficial preparations for our family... and ourselves ... is one of life's *simple* pleasures! The most common herbs can cure common ailments. Take the sage gargle that relieves an irritated throat; cold symptoms mitigated by a concoction of honey and mint; sorrel will soothe bites, as will lavender flowers applied directly on the skin to relieve burns, itching and insect bites.

If we intend to prepare Simples out of season using dried leaves, we need to collect them on a dry day after the morning dew has evaporated. Leaves are best harvested from young shoots up to the time of flowering and care should be taken not to bruise them. Aromatic herbs such as rosemary, sage and peppermint produce a fragrance - and with it their essential oils – in the midday sun and should be cut just before noon when the volatile oil content is at its highest.

Flowers should be harvested when their healing properties are at their best – just after they have opened, in dry weather and before the midday heat. Choose undamaged flowers and pick them with great care, without bruising the petals if possible.

Do not wash the leaves or flowers before drying as they are more likely to develop mould if they are left damp; cut herbs also need to be kept out of direct sunlight as this will spoil their quality and diminish any therapeutic actions. To kill any insect larvae that may be in our fresh herbs – particularly in roots and flower heads – wrap the herb in a polythene bag and place in the freezer for a few days. The frozen larvae will drop off the herb and be caught in the bag. These can be shaken out and discarded before the herb is used.

Endpiece: Never use a plant that is unfamiliar, or if you are not 100% confident of its identity. This particularly applies to those found growing in the wild. The most common problems in herbal treatment are not side effects but misapplication, and the wrong herb may exacerbate a problem. Bear in mind that even some milder herbs can have a cumulative effect and are best taken only for short periods: and avoided altogether during pregnancy.

Tish Romanov at the Old Apothecary had this to say on the subject ...

Not too long ago I was asked to write a piece on the dangers of self-prescribing herbal medicines. We all have some experience in self-prescribing, from the mustard baths that are used to treat tired, stressed muscles, colds and fevers to the age-old remedies of honey and lemon or lemon and ginger used to treat colds and flu. But these are relatively simple remedies with little or no dangers attached.

In recent years the popularity of using alternative medicine has grown exponentially. People are looking for alternatives to conventional medicines for a variety of reasons, conventional medicine may have failed them, the idea of harsh chemical drugs does not appeal, or a desire to return to a simpler, more natural approach to healing the body. Whatever the reason, millions of people around the world have turned to herbal medicine to treat a variety of conditions. Many will tell you that herbal medicine is safe because it comes from plants, and therefore is natural, and couldn't possibly harm you. But are they right? Is herbal medicine safe to use? And if it is safe, why do medical herbalists exist at all? Why not take control of prescribing ourselves?

Herbal medicine has been used by humans for thousands of years. In the UK, we have a long tradition of using herbal Simples, a tradition that is upheld by many rural folks, and by traditional witches who as part of their training learn how to concoct and use ancient Simples. A Simple is a single herb used to treat an ailment on its own. Classic examples of simples include the use of elder flowers to treat coughs, colds and flu, parsley tea to treat urine and kidney infections, parsley poultices for swellings and sores, and peppermint to treat digestive problems including colic and flatulent indigestion.

All of these and many more are known to witches and rural folk, and have been used for generations. However, in this modern age, we in many ways rely on modern pharmaceuticals when we become unwell, and this is a potential mine field when we add herbal medicine into the mix. So too is the new found craze for self-diagnosis and self-prescribing.

The real danger in prescribing legal herbs comes not from potential toxicity in overdose, but rather from drug interactions. Most people these days take a prescription medication and pretty much every prescription medication interacts in some way with herbal medicines.

Chapter Two

Preparation & Usage

The majority of herbs used in domestic plant medicine have a benign action and are considered safe, being only suitable for simple remedies or gentle relief from certain ailments. Much of this use of everyday plants for treating everyday ailments has come down to us from being treated by parents and grandparents by using 'stuff' straight from the garden – particularly amongst country folk. As Gabrielle Hatfield discovered when conducting research for her book – *Memory, Wisdom & Healing: The History of Domestic Plant Medicine* – that much of this has been largely ignored, apart from the Victorian and somewhat patronizing account by W G Black in his *Folk-Medicine: A Chapter on the History of Culture*, published by the Folklore Society in 1883.

> *Much has been written about the recorded plant medicines of the herbals and of the herbalists, but these records omit some of the everyday plant medicines used by our forebears … The use of our common native British plants in everyday home medicine is now almost obsolete; it is a matter of urgency to record the knowledge of such plant usage for posterity. The distilled wisdom of the centuries is something that we should proudly preserve, rather than patronizingly dismiss.*

The problem with this kind of folk-medicine is that it was never properly explained. The ailment was complained about and the 'cure' administered by picking a handful of 'summat' from the garden that was then applied to the injured place, or taken in the form of an infusion, before everything went back to normal. We never bother to ask *what* we were being given, or *why* and any information that we retained was probably because we were usually sent out to pick whatever was needed! Needless to say, we weren't on the wide variety of *chemical* medications as we are today, and the reactions weren't something we needed to be concerned about …

Harvesting

Herbal remedies, like all garden produce, were usually of their season and those that were required for out of season use had to be harvested and correctly prepared to preserve them for the winter. If we consult *The Kitchen & Garden Books of Herbs*, we find a priceless snippet of information:

> *Harvesting the herbs you have grown is a continuous process rather than a one off annual event. Once established, most will grow strongly enough to allow plenty of repeat picking, which in itself encourages new growth in healthy, well-cared for plants.*

The optimum time for harvesting plant material to preserve it for later use depends on the growth pattern of the individual herb and the part of the plant that is to be preserved. Choose the morning of a fine, sunny day so that the essential oil content, which gives the herb its flavour and scent, it as its best. Herbs tend to go mouldy before the drying process is complete if picked when raining. The idea is to preserve the plant before the active constituents start to break down and lose vitality; so, only pick herbs in small quantities and as much as can be dealt with at one time. Even leaving them in small heaps waiting to be processed can encourage heat to build up and deterioration begins to set in.

There are lots of elements in witch-lore concerning the picking of herbs that smack of superstition but when we study them, we find that these are generally items of sound practical advice concerning the constituents of the plants. From what Pliny and other ancient herbal texts tell us, there were definite rituals to be adopted and weather lore to be studied when gathering and 'charging' herbs, which, though differing in minor details, seems to have been consistent throughout Europe; and why, according to the old writers, some herbs are better for being gathered at night, usually around sunset, midnight, or sunrise. The volatile oils of a plant can dissipate in the afternoon heat - hence the instruction to gathering at dusk or in the early morning after the dew has evaporated.

In magical books much is made of the secrecy of collecting plants under the cover of darkness, and the type of blade used to cut them but again there was often a perfectly simple and *practical* explanation for this aside from the magical connotations. All plants are best used fresh but it is necessary to make provision for the out of season times of the year when dried herbs must suffice. The phases of the moon often play an important part in planting and harvesting, so these too needed to be taken into account when collecting herbs, especially those intended for magical use. Iron *can* have a detrimental effect upon the medicinal properties plant if a blade comes in contact with the sap or root; and it has been confirmed by scientific experiment that certain trace elements and minerals found in some plants can be distorted, or even destroyed, by iron. Regardless of what some might think – witches weren't silly!

Drying

It goes without saying that all herbs should be used fresh where possible and those stored for out- of-season use must be properly dried before being put away. The best place to dry leaves is in a warm, dry, dark environment, with most leaves taking about a week to dry completely, although very succulent or very thick leaves may take up to a month. Spread the leaves thinly on clean paper – newspaper is unsuitable since the printer's ink may stain the leaves – or hang them up in small bunches so the air can circulate.

Flowers should retain their colour if dried correctly but will fade if the temperature is too high. Spread on clean paper or muslin, small flowers like chamomile take about a week to dry, while larger flowers like marigold can take up to three weeks to reach perfect dryness. Successful drying depends on removing the moisture in the fresh herb without sacrificing the volatile content. The key to success is creating an environment with the right temperature and low humidity – oven drying is generally too fierce even on the lowest setting.

Storing

Dried herbs and flowers deteriorate quickly, losing aroma and colour if left exposed to light and air. Careful storage will keep most herbs in good condition for up to twelve months or so because the two factors make herbs deteriorate: contamination from the air (moisture, heat and light) and bacteria. The solution is to pack the herbs into airtight containers such as dark glass jars and bottles with tight-fitting lids. A sliver of dry paper will absorb any moisture and keep the contents fresh.

Preserving

Flavouring culinary oils and vinegars with fresh herbs is an easy and useful way to enjoy their flavours right through the winter months. Oils containing fresh herbs can grow harmful moulds if the bottle had been opened and the contents are not full covered by the oil. To prevent this, remove the herb once the flavour has passed to the oil. Heating white wine or cider vinegar is best for steeping woody stemmed herbs like rosemary to make a strong-flavoured herb vinegar that is ready for immediate use with a couple of sprigs of rosemary tips facing uppermost into the bottle. Be warned that an untreated aluminum pan might impart a metallic taste.

Several different herbs can be used for flavour or appearance in ice cubes and added to drinks – such as borage, pineapple mint, and parsley. Put chopped herbs or herb-flowers in ice-cube trays, adding about one tablespoon of water to each tablespoon of herb.

Dried herbs can be obtained from any good herbalist or health shop but do bear in mind that even commercially dried herbs *do* have an expiry date as far as their potency is concerned and should be discarded if over a year old ... or use them for other purposes such as making aromatic sachets for the bath, or for dresser drawers/linen cupboard sachets/bags to add a pleasant scent. Once we are aware of the different properties of the individual herbs we can decide on the best preparations for our needs. Some preparations (compounds) require time and special materials, while others – like those Simple preparations included in this book - *simply* need boiling water.

Infusions

Also referred to as teas or *tisanes* (made famous by Agatha Christie's Hercule Poirot), infusions are water-based extracts of plants, recommended for preparing the delicate parts of a plant, such as flowers, leaves and green stems. They are also used where a mild preparation is required, or for compresses where a mild external application is needed.

Hot infusions are made with water that has been boiled then left to stand for 3 seconds. Use 1 oz of dried herbs or 1½ oz of fresh herb to make one pint of tea. Put the herb into a warmed china or glass teapot – not a metal one – and pour the hot water over it. Cover and steep for 5-10 minutes, depending on the strength required. Strain and sip slowly while hot. Herbal infusions may be sweetened with honey, or flavoured with fresh lemon juice to taste. The standard dose for herbal teas is one cup, two or three times a day for adults, unless stated otherwise. Infusions should be prepared and used immediately. They can be refrigerated for up to two days, but if there is any sign of spoiling, they should be discarded.

Tea Balls

To use a tea infuser – china or plastic but not metal - start by putting 1 to 2 teaspoons of loose herb into the infuser; then, place the infuser in your cup and pour hot water over it. Next, wait 2 minutes for the herb to steep before removing the infuser from the mug. Finally, discard the herb and rinse out the infuser.

Decoctions

Like infusions, decoctions are water-based, but are used for the tough parts of the herbs, such as seeds, barks and roots, that release their active constituents only if cut or broken into small pieces and simmered. To prepare a decoction use 1 oz broken dried herb or 1½ oz chopped fresh herb to make one pint of the decoction. Place the herb into an enamel or stainless steel pan, cover with cold water and a tight-fitting lid. Slowly bring to the boil, then reduce the heat and simmer for 15 minutes. Strain and add water to make up one pint if necessary. Sip slowly while hot and sweeten with honey if desired. The standard dose is half a cup, three times a day, unless stated otherwise. Decoctions will keep for three days if refrigerated but are at their most effective if prepared fresh every day.

- Infusions and decoctions should smell fresh and retain their colour. Too much sediment may be a sign of age.

Compresses and Poultices

To make a compress, soak a clean cotton cloth in an herbal infusion or decoction, place it over the affected part and cover with a clean towel. Keep replacing the compress to keep the area cool or hot as required. For cold compresses cool the liquid before use by making a strong infusion or decoction and adding ice cubes after straining the liquid.

For a poultice, dried or powdered herbs should be blended using hot water and spread onto clean gauze before application to the skin. A couple of drops of olive oil onto the area to be treated will make the removal of the poultice easier. Though practiced for thousands of years, the use of poultices in general medicine fell out of favour before *Fernie's Herbal Simples* had reached its centenary. A poultice is a moist concoction – usually heated – and sometimes known as a 'plaster' when the poultice was smeared on a bandage before application. The most popular seem to have been made of bread, linseed, or mustard mixed with water; the use of bran, flour and starch was also common, or herbs such as comfrey and horseradish root were often added to the mix.

Also called a cataplasm, the paste was made of herbs, plants, and other substances with healing properties; spread on a warm, moist cloth and applied to the body to relieve inflammation and promote healing, held in place with a wide bandage. For making the paste, herbs were usually crushed into a pulp or made into a paste that was spread directly onto the surface of the skin, up to an inch thick, and held in place with gauze or muslin wrapped around the area to keep the poultice from rubbing off. A very basic poultice can even be applied with a whole leaf held in place with an adhesive bandage!

There are several herbs that are classics for making poultices and are well known for their safe and versatile natures. These include: plantain (leaves); chickweed (leaves and stems); cabbage (leaf); calendula (flower petals); dandelion (leaves) and burdock (root).

- Compresses should retain their smell and colour for two days but should be discarded after that time. Poultices should be discarded immediately after use: do not reheat any herbal mixture used for a poultice.

Most of the volatile oils of many culinary herbs are lost during heating, so that their anti-infective properties are greatly diminished. For example, cooking does not affect garlic's cardiovascular properties but it does degrade its antibacterial substances. To preserve these, fresh herbs can be added to a dish *after* it has been taken off the heat. Nevertheless, herbs in the diet can stimulate appetite and digestion and ease the symptoms of trapped wind. Using herbs for cooking is different from taking them medicinally, since the amounts are usually much smaller and heating the herb can lessen its medicinal effect.

Old herbals

Before the invention of the printing press in 1440, herbals were written and illustrated by hand, often copied many times and giving rise to errors and different versions. Early herbals combined myth and magic with the description and practical advice. They contained information that was in itself ancient, and often shows foreign influences that were learned from trade and travel of the time. Although older writings exist which deal with herbal medicine, the major initial works in the field are considered to be the *Edwin Smith Papyrus* in Egypt (c.1600BC); *Pliny's pharmacopoeia*; and *De Materia Medica,* a five-volume book originally written in Greek by Dioscorides. The latter is considered to be precursor to all modern pharmacopoeia, and is one of the most influential herbal books in history. In fact, it remained in use until about1600. A number of early pharmacopoeia books were written by Persian and Arab physicians, including *The Canon of Medicine* of Avicenna in 1025, and works by Ibn Zuhr (Avenzoar) in the 12th-century (and printed in 1491), and Ibn Baytar in the 14th-century.

c.320BCE: *Enquiry into Plants (Historia Plantarum) and Growth of Plants (De Causis Plantotum)* by Theophratus, A total of 500 herbs based on Aristotle's botanical writings, with his own observations in nine books. The ninth book is one of the first herbals, admittedly much simpler than those of Nicander, Dioscorides or Galen, but Theophrastus covers juices (*chylismos*), gums, and resins, the uses of some hundreds of plants as medicines, and how to gather them. He records that apart from Greece itself, medicinal plants are produced in Italy in Tyrrhenia, as Aeschylus records, and Latium; and in Egypt, which as Homer mentions is the source of the drug *nepenthes* that makes men forget sorrow and passion.

c.70CE: *De Materia Medica* by Dioscorides, a Greek physician, pharmacologist and botanist who served with the Roman army in the 1st century, and whose work became the precursor to all modern pharmacopeias that was widely read for more than 1,500 years. The work also records the Dacian, Thracian, Roman, ancient Egyptian and North African (Carthaginian) names for some plants, which otherwise would have been lost.

c77: *Natural History (Historia Naturalis)* by Pliny in thirty-seven volumes of fact and fantasy, including medicinal uses of plants; origin of the Doctrine of Signatures. Pliny made frequent use of Theophrastus, including his books on plants, in his *Natural History*; the only authors he cited more often were Democritus and Marcus Terentius Varro.

c.150: *De Simplicibus* by Galen the Greek physician whose works codified existing medical knowledge and propounded the theory of humours - they were standard medical texts in Europe and the Arab world until the Renaissance. Among the many works on plants from antiquity and the Middle Ages that have come down to us, Galen's treatise *Simple Medicines*, in eleven books, stands out not only because of its length (about a thousand pages), but also because it lays special emphasis on the properties of plants, animals, and minerals used as simple medicines. Instead of merely describing Simples, as many of his predecessors and followers did, Galen devoted five books out of eleven to defining the correct method in using drugs.

c.400: *The Herbal of Apuleius* – author unknown. Originally written in Latin it drew quite heavily on Dioscorides and Pliny, adding pagan prayers and superstitions. It was much copied over the years, including an Anglo-Saxon translation made in 11th century, formerly in the Abbey of Bury St. Edmunds (MS, Bodley 130). The earliest surviving manuscript of this herbal, a codex containing a Latin herbarium and other medical texts, was produced in Southern Italy or Southern France in the sixth or early seventh century. It is preserved in the library of University of Leiden. The *Herbarium Apulei* was one of the most widely used remedy books of the Middle Ages and over sixty medieval manuscripts of the text survive.

c.900: *Leech Book of Bald.* Manual of a Saxon doctor and the earliest European herbal written in the vernacular (also known as *Medicinale Anglicum*) is an Old English medical text probably compiled in the ninth century, possibly under the influence of Alfred the Great's educational reforms. The text survives in only one manuscript, London, British Library Royal MS 12 D XVII.

c.995: *Colloquy (Nominum Herbarrum)* by a Benedictine monk, Aelfric of Cerne Abbas, which comprised a list of over 200 herbs and trees, several of which are no longer identifiable.

c.1000: *Canon of Medicine* by Avicenna, the great physician of the Islamic world. Based on Galen, written in Arabic, translated into Latin, it was a standard text until the 17th century. Book 2 (the *Materia Medica*) of the *Canon* alphabetically lists about 800 'simple' medical substances that were used at the time. The substances are simple in the sense of not being compounded with other substances. The first part gives general rules about drugs and a treatise on what was called 'the science of powers of medicines. The second part is a list of 800 simple floral, mineral, and animal substances. Each entry contains the substance's name, its criteria of goodness (which sometimes describes how the substance is found in nature), and its nature or primary qualities.

c.1150: *Physica* by Hildegard of Bingen. Unique as a book on the medicinal properties of plants by a woman and a great influence on the famous German 'fathers of botany', Brunfels, Fuchs and Hieronymus Bock. In *Physica, Hildegard* presents nine 'books' of healing systems: plants, elements, trees, stones, fish, birds, animals, reptiles, and metals. In each book she discusses the qualities of these natural creations and elaborates on their medicinal use, explaining how to prepare and apply different remedies.

c.1250: *De Proprietatibus* by Bartholomaeus Anglicus in nineteen volumes of natural history – the seventeenth constituting the only original herbal written in England during the Middle Ages; an early forerunner of the encyclopedia and a widely cited book in its time.

c.1234: The *Red Book of Hergest* by the Physicians of Myddfai, who were a succession of herbal physicians who lived in Carmarthenshire, Wales. The first record of them is from the 13th century and the succession continued until 1739, when John Jones, the last of the long line of physicians, died. Their instructions for preparing herbal medicine have survived in the *Red Book of Hergest,* which dates from the late 14th century, and in other, more recent, Welsh manuscripts.

1491: *Hortus Sanitatis* (*The Garden of Health*) compiled by publisher Jacob Meydenbach of Mainz. The last of the medieval works on herbs, it was, a Latin natural history encyclopedia, describing species in the natural world along with their medicinal uses and modes of preparation.

1500: *Liber de Arte Distillandi de Simplicibus* by Hieronymus Braunschweig. The first major work on the techniques of distillation '*of the waters of all manner of herbs*' (English translation by L Andrewes 1527), including:

an enumeration of herbal and animal substances in alphabetical order with botanical remarks on indigenous plants, based on Brunschwig's Braunschweig's own observations. This was followed by the enumeration of indications of the distilled medicines; these indications were based as well as on the writings in the textbooks of old tradition (Dioscorides, etc.) as on prescriptions of folk medicine.

1525: *Banckes' Herbal.* A compilation of earlier herbals, including the 10th century Aemilius Macer's herbal (*De Virtuibus Herbarum*), a poem on the virtues of seventy-seven herbs, and the famous discourse on rosemary sent by the French Countess of Hainault to her daughter, Philippa, Edward I's queen. The first book printed in England, which can really be called a herbal, is an anonymous quarto volume, without illustrations. The title-page runs, '*Here begynneth a newe mater, the whiche sheweth and treateth of ye vertues and proprytes of herbes, the whiche is called an Herball*'.

1530: *Herbarum Vivae Eicones* by Otto Brunfels, a former monk, botanist and physician. Published in Strasbourg, with realistic illustrations, it began the movement towards a more scientific approach to the subject and contains excellent and accurate drawings by the wood engraver Hans Weiditz. This emphasis on accuracy also appeared in the subsequent herbals of Hieronymus Bock and Leonhard Fuchs.

1539: *Kräuter Buch* by Hieronymus Bock. Rather than repeat Dioscorides, Bock wrote about native plants, was the first to attempt a system of plant classification and who began the transition from medieval botany to the modern scientific worldview by arranging plants by their relation or resemblance.

1542: *De Historia Stirpium Commentarii Insignes* by Leonhard Fuchs, in which he tried to identify the plants described by the classical authors. He stocked the garden attached to his house with rare specimens solicited from friends around Europe, and he assembled a large botanical library. The book contains the description of about 400 wild and more than 100 domesticated plant species and their medical uses in alphabetical order. The text is mainly based on Dioscorides and contains 512 pictures of plants (largely growing locally), in woodcuts. Its appeal to gardeners, botanists, bibliophiles, and the casual viewer was immediate, while the clarity of its plant pictures continues to define a standard for botanical illustrators.

1551-68: *A New Herball* (in three parts) by William Turner. The first English herbal with a scientific approach, illustrated with over 400 outstanding woodcuts, mostly reproduced from drawings by Leonhard Fuchs in Swiss herbals. *A New Herball*, originally published in three parts during the second half of the sixteenth century, was the first English herbal with any pretensions to scientific status. As such, it provided a landmark in the history of botany and herbalism, breaking new ground in its accuracy of observation and its scientific thoroughness. For the first time since its original publication, the entire *Herball* is now available in a facsimile edition which faithfully reproduces the beautiful sixteenth-century black-letter text and woodcut illustrations. To aid the twentieth-century reader, a modernised transcript, together with keyed-in notes, a glossary of unfamiliar terms and comprehensive indexes have been provided. Biographical information on this influential physician, naturalist and cleric is also included to give an indication of his contribution to sixteenth-century English history.

1554: *Cruydeboeck* by Rembert Dodoens, a physician to the Holy Roman Emperor Maximillian II and professor of botany at Leyden University. His first herbal, *Cruydeboeck* (1554), was largely derived from the herbal of Leonhart Fuchs, but later compilations began to include plants gathered in his many travels. It was a work of botanical importance, which borrowed Fuch's pictures with many English editions, including *A Niewe Herbal or History of Plants* by Henry Lyte in 1578.

1563: *Coloquios dos Simples* by Garcia de Orta, a Portuguese doctor who spent time in Goa and produced a book on the plants and medicines of India. In general, the drugs are considered in alphabetical order, but with exceptions. Each of the substances that come up for discussion are dealt with fairly systematically: its identification and names in earlier texts, its source, its presence in trade, its medical and other uses.

1569: *Dos libros, el uno que trata de todas las cosas que traen de nuestras Indias Occidentales* by Nicholas Monardes, a Spaniard who never set foot in the Americas. His book on the plants of the 'New World' became better known by the title of the first English edition: *Joyfull Newes Out of the Newe Founde Worlde*, 1577.

1570: *Herbal* by Paracelsus (Theophrastus Bombastus von Hohenheim), a Swiss physician and alchemist who expounded the 'Doctrine of Signatures'. For Paracelsus, the doctrine was the principle upon which to establish a rational knowledge of *materia medica*. It was impossible to understand anything about plants without this knowledge. *'Who writes about the power of the herbs without the signature, is not writing from knowledge. He* *writes like a blind man.'* He is often considered to be the father of alternative medicine in the Western world

1597: *The Herball or Generall Historie of Plants* by John Gerard, the eminent Elizabethan herbalist and gardener. Based on Dodoen's *Cruyboecha* (1554), and extended by Thomas Johnson in 1633; it has delightful descriptions of plants from all over the world. Having trained as a Barber-surgeon, John Gerard divided his time working as superintendent of the gardens of William Cecil, Lord Burghley, as curator of the Physic Garden at the College of Physicians as well as maintaining his own private garden in which he *'grew all manner of strange trees, herbes, rootes, plants, flowers and other such rare things'* including the first potato grown in England. His *Herball*, the most famous of all English herbals, was first published in 1597 and reprinted in 1633 and 1636. It was an instant success and remained influential until the eighteenth century. It also included an extensive commentary with anecdotes on the folklore surrounding certain plant species. The 1636 edition contained over 800 species of plants and more than 2,500 woodcuts.

1598: A Matthioli's edition of ***Dioscorides,*** which was produced in an expanded form in 1598 to take advantage of the plants recently discovered by Europeans in the Americas; Matthioli was able to put American peppers beside Asian peppers long known to the Greeks and Romans. His updating of the record continued a long Classical tradition of botanical and medical works that strove to keep up with the latest introductions to the Mediterranean world from Asia and Africa.

1629: *Paradisi in Sole Paradisus Terrestris; Theatrum Botnicum* 1640 by John Parkinson. The latter is the largest herbal in English. Less known than the former, which is more of a gardening book, describing 3800 herbs, divided in seventeen groups, though one group consists of 'straglers' the author had omitted to include elsewhere. This work has been selected by scholars as being culturally important and is part of the knowledge base of civilization as we know it - and is still available in a facsimile edition.

1652: *The English Physitian* by Nicholas Culpeper. One of the best-selling herbals of all time, containing astrological, and often flippant descriptions of 398 herbs. It promoted the Doctrine of Signatures and was castigated as 'ignorant' by physicians of the day. The *English Physitian Enlarged* came out in 1653, followed by many later revisions, including the better-known *Culpeper's Complete Herbal*. He produced an English translation of the medical fraternity's bible, the *Pharmacopoeia Londoninensis*, and while this contained the recipes for their remedies, Nicholas's translation, *A Physical Directory*, also set out the common names of the 'Simples' and how to administer them.

1656: *The Art of Simpling* by William Coles. An introduction to the knowledge and gathering of plants, including an introduction to the gathering of plants wherein the definitions, divisions, places, descriptions, differences, names, virtues, times of flourishing and gathering, uses, temperatures, signatures and appropriations of plants are methodically laid down, including the first account of herbs for treating animals. He is known for the doctrine of signatures of medicinal herbs or 'Simples', whereby the plant has some attribute which shows the botanist what its use may be.

1694 *The Compleat Herbal of Physical Plants* by John Pechey was a more orthodox medical practitioner and a member of London's Royal College of Physicians but he clearly intended his herbal for a literate, but non-medical readership. In his preface, he wrote that he hoped his book would be '*serviceable to Families* *in the Country that are far distant form Physicians'*. The book is available in a facsimile edition from Forgotten Books.

1710: *Botanologia: The English Herbal or History of Plants* by William Salmon. The last major herbal before the discipline of botany and medicine parted company. Like most herbals, entries included names of plants, varieties, descriptions, where the plant grew, its qualities (e.g., hot or cold, dry or wet), its virtues, when it flowered, how to combine it with other ingredients to make medicines, and a list of ailments it was supposed to cure. Entries were also illustrated, showing the different forms of the plant.

1838: *Flora Medica* by John Lindley. A worldwide survey of medicinal plants, written by an eminent botanist and horticulturalist, typical of the new scientific approach; a botanical account of all the more important plants used in medicine in different parts of the world. Available in a facsimile edition by Forgotten Books.

1897: *Herbal Simples Approved for Modern Uses of Cure*, by William Thomas Fernie. The most comprehensive classic encyclopedia of healing *herbs* from A to Z and the most plagiarized on-line herbal of all time without any accreditation. Should be on everyone's shelf as a reference book.

1931: *A Modern Herbal* by Mrs. M Grieve. Second perhaps only to Culpeper's herbal in its popularity, it describes over 1000 herbs. First published in 1931, by Maud Grieve, it contains medicinal, culinary, cosmetic and economic properties, including cultivation and the folk-lore of herbs.

2007: *Hatfield's Herbal* by Gabrielle Hatfield and an excellent companion to *Memory, Wisdom & Healing; The History of Domestic Plant Medicine*, this modern herbal is a valiant attempt to preserve the folk knowledge of our native wild plants since our collective memory of plant remedies is fading as we become an increasingly urban culture. Packed with stories and memorable information these books are the highly personal, very readable result of a life-time spent researching folk cures and the science behind them.

~~~~~~~~~~~~~~~~~~~~~~~~~~~~~~~

As well as the learned texts written by the medical men of their day, there is also a long tradition of more homely recipe (usually spelt 'receipt') books, which include instructions on the culinary and cosmetic use of herbs as well as medicinal remedies. They are sometimes referred to as 'stillroom books' since during the 17th and 18th centuries all the big country houses had their own stillrooms and the lady of the house was supposed to be fully conversant in the art of making herbal and culinary preparations. A stillroom book was simply a notebook in which health, healing, and medicinal information was recorded, and since the good *châtelaine* was expected to be very wise in the preparation and use of the herbs she grew, a stillroom book preserved family herbal Simples for future generations.

Recipes would have been written down and kept in a book in the kitchen to be used over and over again. The stillroom book had a character all its own; it was more than a cook book, less than a herbal, but it contained the accumulated knowledge of the virtues and preparation of the plants, which formed such an important part of the domestic economy of the day. The lady of the house needed to be skilled in the preparation of medicines for the health of the household and must have the knowledge of all sorts of herbs belonging to the kitchen [The 17th-Century Stillroom]

Endpiece: Infusions and decoctions can also be useful in preparing magical cleansing and protective sprays for the home. Herbs and flowers from the kitchen garden and surrounding countryside were infused or distilled, or brewed as required to make rose water, lavender water, tincture and a wide variety of medicines. One of the favourite recipes used in the *still-room* was 'Essence of lavender' and lavender water that was featured in *Country Life Illustrated* in 1899 and required four ounces of lavender flowers that were blended with '*rectified spirit*' and rose water. Or:

> *Elder-flower water was also largely made as a cooling wash for the face and ... eyes made from 9 lbs of elder flowers, free from stalks, and introduce it to the still with four gallons of water; the first three gallons that come over is all that need be preserved for use; 1 oz of 'rectified spirit' should be added to each gallon of water distilled, and when bottled it is ready for use.*

It is now possible to purchase a modern 'still' for distilling and refining plant extracts for herbal or medicinal purposes that looks like an old-fashioned pressure cooker. It is also possible to obtain glass spray bottles that are perfect for magical infusions, as plastic can often absorb smells and retain psychic residue. For magical preparations a family-sized china or glass teapot should hold sufficient liquid for our needs.

Room infusions and/or decoctions should be made from herbs that have protective or cleansing properties (such as bay, broom; chamomile; chervil or garlic) and should be discarded after a magical working, although the liquid can be kept in the fridge for two-three days if a repeating ritual is thought necessary. Room sprays can also be created to aid sleep, from plants such as agrimony, lavender and chamomile. *Spray* in the air around your home to boost your magical application and enhance the ambiance.

Chapter Three

The Simples

Many of the herbs mentioned by the early herbalists like Culpeper had toxic qualities but most of the ones included among the following Simples are safe to use **in the manner in which they are recommended**. Simples were not intended for long-term use and were grown and picked to be used as required in domestic folk-medicine for common ailments such as headaches, upset stomachs, insect bites, splinters, etc., in the form of infusions and compresses.

Nevertheless, some of the herbs listed below now require special warnings although none of them are dangerous in and of themselves ... but if they are combined with the modern penchant for pharmaceutical drugs, there can be potentially fatal consequences. It is actually the pharmaceutical drugs that are dangerous, and care should be taken to ensure that none of these side effects occur. A medical professional should be consulted by anyone taking prescription drugs before embarking on any treatment involving herbal remedies.

According to The Old Apothecary, however, in two cases - comfrey and honey - the danger does lie with the herb. Comfrey is currently undergoing in-depth research as there have been reports of severe liver damage; however, most medical herbalists are happy to prescribe it.

I would suggest that people are very, very careful about using comfrey internally, and would not recommend that they use it in this way without taking professional advice. In the case of honey, babies can develop infant botulism if they are given honey, and this can be fatal, so I would advise that people do not provide it to infants under twelve-months.

Anything more complex should only be administered under the direction of a qualified herbalist or pharmacist. If you haven't used herbal remedies before, infusions can be a great way to benefit from herbs in small doses; and these can be obtained from local health shops to try before growing and preparing your own home-grown remedies. Most herbs in the Simples garden also had their magical uses and these have been included for interest's sake …

As most of my readers will know, the author also has a fascination for odd and obscure historical facts and country-lore that are hidden away in the millions of sources that outstrip and confound the confines of the Internet – it's finding them that presents the stimulation and the challenge. If we merely rely on the regurgitated information of contemporary paganism not only does our mind become stagnant, but for those who follow the Craft of the witch, so do our magical abilities. So, superstitions, folklore and history – and a few personal observations - have also been included just for fun.

~~~~~~~~~~~~~~~~~~~~~~~~~~~~

ACORN

Scientific Name(s): *Quercus robur*
Common Name(s): British Oak; oak nuts;

The Common, or British Oak, for many centuries the chief forest tree of England, has been intimately bound up with the history of these islands from Druidic times. The acorn was esteemed by Dioscorides and other Classic authors, for its supposed medicinal values. As an article of food, it is not known to have been habitually used at any time by the inhabitants of Britain, though acorns furnished the chief support of the large herds of swine on which our forefathers subsisted. The right of maintaining these swine in the woods was called 'panage' and formed a valuable property. [Fernie, *Herbal Simples*] Once a staple food for various societies, acorns are not as frequently consumed today, and while raw acorns harbor high amounts of potentially harmful plant compounds called tannins, properly cooked they are low in tannins and generally safe to eat. In fact, people have been safely consuming acorns for thousands of years. Additionally, acorns have long been used as a herbal remedy to treat stomach pain, bloating, nausea, diarrhoea, and other common digestive complaints. A motif in Roman architecture, also popular in Celtic and Scandinavian art, the acorn symbol was used as an ornament on cutlery, furniture, and jewellery; it also appears on finials in Westminster Abbey and used as charges in heraldry. Carved wooden acorns were also used on blind cords to deter lightning and the nut carried for good luck.

Simple: A decoction of acorns can be made into a room spray to attract good luck and dispel negative energies.

Magical use: The acorn is a symbol of strength and power as well as perseverance and hard work. Acorns have long been used in magic and witchcraft; while ancient folklore tells of carrying acorns to attract prosperity, luck and health.

Superstition and folklore: In parts of Europe, it was customary to place acorns in the hands of the newly dead.

Personal note: The Celts, Romans, Greeks, and Teutonic tribes all had legends connected to the mighty oak; in particular it was associated with deities that had control over thunder, lightning and storms.

AGRIMONY

Scientific Name(s): *Agrimonia eupatoria* L.

Common Name(s): Cocklebur; liverwort; stickwort; Church Steeples;

According to Fernie, agrimony was a Simple well known to all country folk, and used to be abundant throughout England in the fields and woods as a popular domestic herb. It is a perennial plant with small, star-shaped yellow flowers and known as a herb of protection. Agrimony is also used in folk-magic charms to ensure restful sleep. It is especially used when a person is anxious or troubled by nightmares. A traditional English rhyme says of the plant:

> *If it be leyd under mann's head,*
> *He shal sleepyn as he were dead;*
> *He shal never drede ne wakyn*
> *Til fro under his head it be takyn.*

Both the flowers and leaves give off a faint lemony scent and the English used it to make a 'spring' or 'diet' drink for purifying the blood. It was considered especially useful as a tonic for aiding the recovery from winter colds and fevers. It can be hung indoors, in bunches, as a traditional air freshener.

Simple: Use as a bedtime tea or gargle for a sore throat and mouthwash, and externally as a mild antiseptic and astringent. Steep 1 teaspoon dried root, leaves or flowers in 1 cup of boiling water for 15 minutes; strain and flavor with honey if required. Use as a room spray to aid sleep.

CAUTION: DO NOT use if you are Diabetic as agrimony interferes with diabetes medications.

Magical use: In magic the herb is used for protection, either dried in sachet form or as a room-spray.

Superstition and folklore: Add dried agrimony to dream pillows in order to get a good night's sleep.

Personal Note: Agrimony was one of the most famous vulnerary herbs. The Anglo-Saxons, who called it *garclive*, taught that it would heal wounds, snake bites, warts, etc. In the time of Chaucer, when we find its name appearing in the form of *egrimoyne,* it was used with mugwort and vinegar for '*a bad back and alle woundes*'. [Maud Grieve]

ANEMONE, WOOD

Scientific Name(s): *Anemone nemorosa*
Common Name(s): Crowfoot; windflower; Smell Fox;

The Wood Anemone is one of the earliest spring flowers, and one of the most faithful indicators of ancient woodland, rarely extending its territory beyond its ancient traditional sites. In sunshine, the flower is expanded wide, but at the approach of night, it closes and droops its graceful head so that the dew may not settle on it and injure it. If rain threatens in the daytime, it does the same, receiving the drops upon its back, whence they trickle of harmlessly from the sepal tips, and it was said by country-folk, the fairies nestled for protection, having first pulled the curtains round them. In the first century AD, Dioscorides recommended the plant to be used in external treatments for eye inflammation and ulcers. The old herbalists referred to it as the 'wood crowfoot', because its leaves resemble in shape of some species of crowfoot. Though this species of anemone has practically fallen out of use, the older herbalists recommended application of various parts of the plant for headaches, tertian agues and rheumatic gout. Culpeper practically copied verbatim some half-dozen uses of the anemone that Gerard gives, saying:

> *The body being bathed with the decoction of the leaves cures the leprosy: the leaves being stamped and the juice snuffed up the nose purgeth the head mightily; so doth the root, being chewed in the mouth, for it procureth much spitting and bringeth away many watery and phlegmatic humours, and is therefore excellent for the lethargy.... Being made into an ointment and the eyelids annointed with it, it helps inflammation of the eyes. The same ointment is excellent good to cleanse malignant and corroding ulcers.*

A large colony of anemones can fill the air with a sharp, musky smell, which is hinted at in some of the old local names such as 'smell fox'.

Simple: None – *'Though so innocent in appearance, the Wood Anemone possesses all the acrid nature of its tribe and is bitter to the tongue and poisonous'*. [*Maud Grieve*]

Magical use: The Romans plucked the first anemones as a charm against fever, and in some remote districts this practice long survived, it being considered a certain cure to gather an anemone saying: *'I gather this against all diseases'*, and to tie it round the invalid's neck.

Superstition and folklore: In some European countries it is looked on by the peasants as a flower of ill-omen, though the reason of the superstition is obscure.

Personal note: The Egyptians held the anemone as the emblem of sickness, perhaps from the flush of colour upon the backs of the white sepals. The Chinese call it the 'Flower of Death'.

ANGELICA

Scientific Name(s): *Angelica archangelica*
Common Names): Holy-ghost root; archangel root; masterwort;

Praised by Paracelsus as a *'marvellous medicine'*, angelica was thought in ancient times to be a panacea for all ills and every part of the plant had health-giving properties. Herbalists valued it as a tonic and as a remedy for coughs and colds. Culpeper recommended that the powered root to be taken as 'angelica water' to resist poison and the plague. Only the seeds and roots are used in medicines.

In Couriand, Livonia and the low lakelands of Pomerania and East Prussia, wild-growing Angelica abounds; there, in early summertime, it has been the custom among the peasants to march into the towns carrying the Angelica flower-stems and to offer them for sale, chanting some ancient ditty in Lettish words, so antiquated as to be unintelligible even to the singers themselves. The chanted words and the tune are learnt in childhood, and may be attributed to a survival of some pagan festival with which the plant was originally associated. [A Modern Herbal]

Crystallized strips of young angelica stems and midribs are green in colour and are sold as decorative and flavor-some cake decoration material, but may also be enjoyed on their own.

Simple: Angelica tea (water) was used to stimulate the appetite, calm digestive disorders and relieve flatulence, or 'corrupt air'. To make angelica tea, add one cup of boiling water to one teaspoon of dried angelica and steep covered for at least ten minutes. Some alternative practitioners suggest drinking one third of a cup of angelica tea thirty minutes before each meal.

Magical use: Featuring in pagan rituals, angelica was grown in England during the Anglo-Saxon period as it was reputed to possess angelic or heavenly powers; a necklace of angelica leaves was worn as a protection against evil spells and witchcraft. All parts of the plant were believed efficacious against spells and enchantment. Grow angelica on your property to protect your garden and home because 'angelica water' is excellent for banishing, healing, and protection; and sprayed around a home to protect the house and those within from baneful magic.

Superstition and folklore: Its virtues are praised by old writers, and the name itself, as well as the folk-lore of all North European countries, testifies to the great antiquity of a belief in its merits as a protection against contagion, for purifying the blood, and for curing every conceivable malady. [*Maud Grieve*]

Personal Note: *Angelica* is truly a useful herb, but accurate identification is crucial since it resembles *water* hemlock, a deadly poisonous plant found in the same habitat. When in doubt purchase from a reputable herbalist or health shop.

ANISEED

Scientific Name(s): *Pimpinella anisum*
Common Name(s): Anise;

The main use of anise in traditional European herbal medicine was for its carminative effect (reducing flatulence), as noted by John Gerard in his *Great Herball*, an early encyclopedia of herbal medicine:

> *The seed wasteth and consumeth winde, and is good against belchings and upbraidings of the stomacke, alaieth gripings of the belly, provoketh urine gently, maketh abundance of milke, and stirreth up bodily lust: it staieth the laske (diarrhoea), and also the white flux (leukorrhea) in women.*

According to Pliny the Elder, anise was used as a cure for sleeplessness, chewed with alexanders and a little honey in the morning to freshen the breath, and, when mixed with wine, as a remedy for asp bites. In 19th-century medicine, anise was prepared as *aqua anisi* (Water of Anise) in doses of an ounce or more and as *spiritus anisi* (Spirit of Anise) in doses of 5–20 minims [*Britannica* 1911]. In Turkish folk medicine, its seeds have been used as an appetite stimulant, tranquilizer, or diuretic. In 1305, King Edward I declared anise a taxable drug and the revenue earned through its import helped repair damages to the London Bridge. The seed (fruit) and oil, and less frequently the root and leaf, were used to make medicine. Anise is used for upset stomach, intestinal gas, runny nose, and as an expectorant to increase productive cough, as a diuretic to increase urine flow, and as an appetite stimulant.

Simple: Place 1 teaspoon of dried *anise* leaf or 3 teaspoons of fresh, crushed *anise* leaf or leaves into one cup of boiling water. Allow to steep for a few minutes. It is now ready to serve to aid digestion.

Magical use: Anise aids in divination and may be added to a ritual bath and/or burned while meditating or divining.

Superstition and folklore: Anise was one of the ingredients in the ancient Roman *mustaceus*, a special cake made with digestive herbs that was served as a finishing dish for feasts as a digestive and may be the origin of the modern-day wedding cake.

Personal note: Anise can be made into a liquid scent and is used for both drag hunting and fishing. It is put on fishing lures to attract fish.

APPLE (see also Crab Apple)

Scientific Name(s): *Malus spp*
Common Name(s): Wildings; crab apple;

'An apple a day keeps the doctor away' and helps to reduce cholesterol and stabilise blood sugar naturally. Apples are also useful to the digestion in regulating bowel movements and are traditionally believed to aid the digestion of fatty foods, hence the custom of serving apple sauce with roast pork. Cultivated varieties of apple were probably introduced into England by the Romans. During medieval times, monks increased the number of varieties by grafting scions (shoots) brought from other monasteries on to established rootstocks. They may be small and sour, but the fruit of the crab apple has an exceptionally high pectin and acid content which makes them ideal for setting fruit jams and jellies. Bartholomeus Anglicus, whose *Encyclopedia* was one of the earliest printed books containing botanical information (being printed at Cologne about 1470), gives a chapter on the apple. He says:

Malus the Appyll tree is a tree yt bereth apples and is a grete tree in itself. . . it is more short than other trees of the wood wyth knottes and rinelyd Rynde. And makyth shadowe wythe thicke bowes and branches: and fayr with dyurs blossomes, and floures of swetnesse and Iykynge: with goode fruyte and noble. And is gracious in syght and in taste and vertuous in medecyne . . . some beryth sourysh fruyte and harde, and some ryght soure and some ryght swete, with a good savoure and mery.

In old hedgerows crab apple trees can be conspicuous landscape features, especially when in blossom, and they are the third most mentioned species as boundary features in Anglo-Saxon and Welsh charters. [*Flora Britannica*]

Simple: To make the most of all the beneficial effects of apples they are best eaten fresh and unpeeled. A glass of fresh apple juice can be a quick remedy for nausea (morning sickness).

Magical use: The apple is the 'goddess tree' and all parts of it can be used in spell-casting for attracting love and romance. If you *cut* the apple horizontally, both halves will reveal a *pentagram*.

Superstition and folklore: The apple tree and its fruit have been the center of superstitions and magical folklore for centuries. A tree of the Faere Folk - to cut down a living apple tree will bring nothing but bad luck and misfortune.

Personal Note: A traditional recipe for mulled cider with crab apple is splendidly autumnal and even has a traditional country name, 'lambswool', because of the fluffy apple puree that bursts from the fruit and floats on top.

BARLEY

Scientific Name(s): *Hordeum vulgare*

Common Name(s): John Barleycorn; barleykerne; aleseed; pearl barley;

Barley has been cultivated as a cereal crop as far back as

Neolithic times. The grains have been discovered in ancient Egyptian remains, while the Greeks considered the seeds to be sacred; Ceres was the Roman goddess of the harvest and was credited with teaching humans how to grow, preserve, and prepare grain and corn. Ale, made of malted barley (seeds that have germinated), was a staple drink in medieval monasteries, while pearl barley (seeds that have had the husks removed) was cooked in soups and stews.

Simple: Barley water soothes digestive inflammations, aids weight loss, lowers blood sugar levels and cholesterol. Cooked barley, applied externally in the form of a poultice, was used to treat skin sores. A daily glass of barley water helps flush out toxins from the body and the intestines through the urinary tract and it's easy to make. Some choose to add natural flavorings, such as lemon and honey, to the water to give it a better taste. And to make six cups of lemon barley water, we need:

¾ cup of pearl barley
2 lemons (juice and peel)
½ cup of honey
6 cups of water

Rinse the barley under cold water until water runs clear; put the barley in a saucepan, along with lemon peel and six cups of water. Bring the mixture to the boil over a medium heat. Turn down the heat and simmer for between 15 and 30 minutes. Strain the mixture into a heatproof bowl and discard the barley; stir in the honey until it dissolves. Pour into bottles and refrigerate until chilled.

Magical use: Barley is one of the great grains of the world, and the one most closely associated with the sacrificial grain god. It is a Lammas plant, planted late and harvested early - and used in Lammas altar sheaves. Cut a bunch from the edge of the barley field and keep the dried stalks in a large vase in thanks for the harvest.

Superstition and folklore: The 'corn spirit' of the barley is a common theme throughout northern Europe and translated into the 'spirit' (brandy) distilled from the grain.

Personal Note: 'Rigs O' Barley' used in *The Wicker Man* film is from a lyric by Robert Burns.

BASIL

Scientific Name(s): *Ocimum basilicum*
Common Name(s): Albahaca; sweet basil;

A native of south-east Asia, basil has been cultivated in Europe from at least Roman times. Because it releases its scent when walked upon, it was a useful herb for strewing on floors to cover offensive smells. Fresh basil seasoned medieval sauces, soups and drinks and although versatile, it is one of the few herbs that *increases* its flavor when cooked, and should be used sparingly. Basil is now mainly used for cooking but for many centuries it was a very important medicinal plant across the world. The fresh leaves (far superior to the dried) can be eaten regularly in salads as a nerve tonic and fresh plants can be bought weekly from the supermarket. Used as a relief from insect bites, the itching can be relieved by the compounds of camphor and thymol within basil leaves.

Simple: 1-3 fresh leaves intake per day will suffice.
Magical use: Basil was used in English folk magic, like so many other things, to ward off harmful spells as well as to keep away pests. *Holy basil* has been grown and used in India for over 3,000 years where it's often referred to as *Tulsi*, or the Incomparable One, and considered one of the most *sacred* of herbs.
Superstition and folklore: Bunches of basil hung in the kitchen reputedly repel flies.

Personal Note: The general observances are entirely at variance with the idea prevailing among the ancient Greeks that the herb represented hate and misfortune. The Romans believed that the more the plant was abused, the better it would prosper.

BAY

Scientific Name(s): *Laurus noblis*
Common Name(s): Sweet Bay; True Laurel; Laurier d'Apollon; Roman Laurel; Noble Laurel; Lorbeer; Daphne;

Bay can be grown as an ornamental tree as well as a pot herb. The leaves are popular as a flavouring for sauces and one or two leaves used in stews and soups helps to strengthen digestion. *Boil* or steam fresh foods with *bay leaves* to enhance the natural flavor. Bay leaves are used fresh, and may be gathered all the year round to provide protection in the home; make a room spray from a decoction of bay leaves and crush a fresh leaf in door and window catches to repel negative energy.

Simple: Make a *decoction* of 4-5 *bay leaves* in 1 litre of water to use as a room spray. Boil for 10 minutes, strain and leave to cool, Keep in a glass spray bottle in the refrigerator.

CAUTION: DO NOT take bay leaf as a medicine if you have been prescribed the following medications: meperidine (Demerol), hydrocodone, morphine, OxyContin, clonazepam (Klonopin), lorazepam (Ativan), phenobarbital (Donnatal), zolpidem (Ambien), as serious side effects may occur.

Magical use: Considered the plant of metamorphosis and illumination, bay leaf is the symbol of divine wisdom. Its scent can bring the mind to rise on subtle planes and awaken inspiration by urging the inner expression of creativity. Burn bay leaves to banish negative thought by writing what you wish to get rid of in marker pen; hold the leaf by the stem over a candle and letting it burn. Bay is sacred to Apollo.

Superstition and folklore: During the Middle Ages bay was used as a strewing herb, valued not only for it scent but also as an insect repellant.

Personal Note: The leaves were also used for the crowning wreaths to honour heroes in ancient Greece and Rome. The Delphic priestesses are said to have made use of the leaves.

BEECH

Scientific Name(s): *Fagus sylvatica*
Common Name(s): Common beech;

Listed by Aelfric, the beech was established at least 1,000 years before Julius Caesar wrongly stated that there were no beech trees in England. In medieval times pigs were often turned out in the autumn to forage on the fallen beech mast. The sap of the tree was tapped and fermented to be made into wine and ale; oil from the seeds was used for cooking, while the seeds were roasted. According to *Organic Facts*, beech tree leaves and shoots have been eaten for hundreds (if not thousands) of years, particularly in times of famine. The high cellulose and fiber content is good for regulating digestion and offers a viable 'foraging food' if that becomes necessary on hikes, camping trips, etc.

Simple: To alleviate sprains and swellings the leaves can also be boiled down to create a poultice with proven analgesic properties. The leaves should be boiled and mashed before placing direct onto the skin and held in place with a piece of clean linen and bandage.

Magical use: Because its copper-yellow *leaves* fall only when new *leaves* begin to sprout, it symbolizes transformation. It is the sacred tree of learning and is used while working with the Ancestors, old wisdom, and magical research.

Superstition and folklore: It is also associated with wishes, where one folk magical tradition has a person write their wish on a beech stick, then bury the stick in the ground. Superstition also suggests that beech wood or leaves can be carried to enhance the flow of creativity.

Personal Note: Psithurism comes from the Greek word *psithuros*, which means 'whispering', which certainly fits with the sound wind often makes when it blows through trees – especially beech leaves in winter.

BEET

Scientific Name(s): *Beta*
Common Name(s): Table beet; mangel wurzel; garden beet; sea beet; dinner beet or golden beet;

Beets have been cultivated in England at least since Anglo Saxon times. Beetroot is of exceptional nutritional value, especially the green leaves, which are rich in calcium, iron and vitamins A and C. Beetroot is an excellent source of folic acid and a very good source of fibre, manganese and potassium. The green leaves should not be overlooked – they can be cooked up and enjoyed in the same way as spinach. The Romans also consumed beetroot for stamina and used the leaves for healing wounds.

Simple: Beetroot provides a wide range of possible health benefits, such as reducing blood pressure, improving digestion, and lowering the risk of diabetes. A 2019 review of studies found that certain compounds in beets can disrupt the cancerous mutations of cells. Such compounds include betalains, which are pigments that give beets their red and yellow color. Although further research is necessary before health professionals can recommend beets as a replacement for other standard cancer risk reduction methods, they may have some function in reducing the risk of this condition if included in the diet. [*Medical News Today*]
Magical use: The beetroot has a really earthy flavour so they work well for grounding and keep us connected with Mother Earth. Beets also help heal old wounds from the past.

Superstition and folklore: Gardeners were convinced that root crops, such as potatoes, beets, carrots, etc. must be planted in the dark of the moon, while beans, peas, lettuce, and other above-ground crops need to be planted when the moon was full, or nearly so.

Personal Note: Ancient Greeks cultivated beetroot around 300 BC but they didn't use the roots of the plant and only ate the leaves. They nevertheless respected the root and offered it to the god Apollo in the temple of Delphi. They also considered it to be worth its weight in silver.

BETONY

Scientific Name(s): *Stachys officinalis*
Common Name(s): Bishopswort; woundwort; hedge nettle;

It is a pretty woodland plant, found frequently throughout England, but by no means common in Scotland. Though generally growing in woods and copses, it is occasionally to be found in more open situations, and amongst the tangled growths on heaths and moors. Betony has traditionally been used to treat a huge range of complaints: Augustus Caesar's physician listed no less than 47 diseases for which it was effective. Like yarrow, betony was widely used as a herb for treating wounds; a compress is helpful for minor cuts and bruises, and for bites and stings, and skin irritations.

Simple: Prepare the compress-infusion by pouring a cup of boiling water on 1-2 teaspoonfuls of the dried herb. Let the herb steep into the water for ten to fifteen minutes before straining and applying as a compress.

Magical use: It was believed to have powerful magical properties and was used for protection against the evil eye and bodily harm; and to bring beautiful and prophetic dreams. It dispels negative energy and eases both internal and external conflicts.

Superstition and folklore: The herb is said to 'protect man from nocturnal visitors and frightful dreams'- or in other words, prevents nightmare.

Personal Note: Held in high repute not only in the Middle Ages, but also by the Greeks who extolled its qualities. An old Italian proverb: *Sell your coat and buy Betony*, and *He has as many virtues as Betony*, is a saying of the Spaniards to show what value was placed on its remedial properties.

BIRCH

Scientific Name(s): *Betula pendula*
Common Name(s): Lady of the Woods; silver birch;

This tree has been a boon to people in the cold north for thousands of years. Its medicinal properties have been historically valued and should be better known today. Called the oldest tree in Britain, birch was a pioneer species when the ice caps retreated, moving in on the devastated land, growing quickly and then rotting to produce a more fertile earth in which other species could take over. Birch has a multitude of historical uses but is less familiar for its undoubted medicinal properties. The sap makes a clear and refreshing drink that can be preserved as a wine, beer, or spirit. The leaves produce a pleasant tea. In each form, birch is an excellent tonic and detoxifier, mainly working on the urinary system to remove waste products, as in kidney or bladder stone, gravel, gout, and rheumatism. It reduces fluid retention and swellings, and clears up many skin problems.

Simple: Brew birch tea by cutting about a quart of twigs into one-inch pieces. Place in a suitable pan and pour hot (but not boiling) water over them. Let the mixture steep until it's cool and strain the twigs and impurities from the water with a fine tea strainer. Heat again and serve warm with milk and a dash of honey.

CAUTION: Birch is a natural diuretic. Taking birch along with other 'water pills' like furosemide may cause your body to lose too much water. This can make you feel dizzy and cause your blood pressure to go too low.

Magical use: Birch is associated with purification, protection, and banishing, and represents renewal, rebirth, and beginnings as it is the first tree after winter to come into leaf. Ideal for a purification/protection spray within the home.

Superstition and folklore: Revered as sacred by the Celts, the tree was believed to drive out evil spirits – hence the birching of wrongdoers and the insane.

Personal Note: During medieval times a bundle of birch rods carried before a magistrate on his way to court symbolized both his authority and a means of correction.

BLACKBERRY

Scientific Name(s): *Rubus fructicosus*
Common Name(s): Bramble; Bumble-Kite; bly; brummel; brameberry; scaldhead; brambleberry;

The Blackberry, or Bramble, growing in every English hedge-row, is too well known to need description. Its blossom, as well as its fruit, both green and ripe, may be seen on the bush at the same time, a somewhat unusual feature, not often met with in other plants. The name of the bush is derived from *brambel*, or *brymbyl*, signifying prickly. The leaves are said to be still in use in England as a remedy for burns and scalds; formerly their operation was helped by a spoken charm. 'Blackberrying, I suspect, carried with it a little of the urban dweller's myth of country life: harvest, a sense of season, and just enough discomfort to quicken the senses,' wrote Richard Mabey in *Flora Britannica*.

Simple: As a remedy for diarrhoea, a gargle for throat inflammations, and a compress for wounds and rashes. For an infusion, put 1 heaped teaspoon of *blackberry leaf* into an infuser. Pour boiled water over the *leaf and* allow to steep for 5 minutes or so in a covered cup. Remove infuser and add honey if required.

Magical use: Blackberry leaves are typically used to remove evil spirits from a home and to return evil to enemies and to protect against those doing you harm.

Superstition and folklore: Across the British Isles it was believed and possibly still believed, that eating blackberries after 11th October was deemed a bad idea because after Old Michaelmas Day they become the Devil's fruit

Personal Note: Though this superstition sounds daft, the truth behind the myth is that cooler wet autumn weather can cause certain molds to start growing on the fruit and may make it toxic. Once again, old fashioned stuff isn't always silly!

BLACKTHORN

Scientific Name(s): *Prunus spinosa*
Common Name(s): Sloe; bullace; (French) *Sibarelles;*

Archaeological research reveals that the fruit of the blackthorn (sloes) were consumed in large quantities as far back as Neolithic times. 'It is a remarkable fact that there is always, that is every year of our lives, a spell of cold and angry weather just at the time this hardy little tree is in bloom. The country people call it the Black Thorn winter and thus it has been called, I dare say, by all the inhabitants of this island, from generation to generation, for a thousand years', comments Richard Mabey in *Flora Britannica.* Later, the purple-black juice, obtained by stabbing the point of a pen into the raw sloe, was used as a marking ink on linen and cloth. Blackthorn flowers were used as a tonic and mild laxative; the leaves as a mouthwash and to stimulate the appetite; the bark to reduce fever; and the fruit for bladder, kidney and digestive disorders. The bitter sloes were made into jellies, syrups, jams, wines and verjuice – and that best of all 'rescue remedies': sloe gin,

Simple: The *leaves* are traditionally used to prepare an herbal *infusion* and used to treat throat ailments such as laryngitis and tonsillitis – or to use as a mouthwash.

Magical use: The blackthorn is a tree of profound magical tradition which can be used for overcoming adversity, banishing negativity, raising awareness and energy, purification, protection, banishing and cursing.

Superstition and folklore: The blackthorn is depicted in many fairytales throughout Europe as a tree of ill omen. Called *Straif* in the Ogham, this tree has the most sinister reputation in Celtic tree lore.

Personal Note: Wintry weather known as 'blackthorn winter' originating in rural England when the confusingly-named white blackthorn blossom blooms in the hedgerows and mimics the springtime snow or frosts in the adjoining fields in advance of the whitethorn that flowers around *Beltaine*. Blackthorn flowers on the bare branches of the tree, while whitethorn flowers against the new, green leaves.

BORAGE

Scientific Name(s): *Borago officinalis*
Common Name(s): Star flower;

Dioscordes, a Roman army physician and author of the famous herbal *Materia Medica*, wrote that the herb *'cheers the heart and raise the spirits'*. Herbalists today use it to alleviate symptoms of stress and as an anti-depressant. The blue star-shaped flowers can be used to flavour summer drinks and the young leaves added to salads. Traditionally borage has been used to treat inflammation of the digestive tract, but has also found a place in the treatment of depression and nervous exhaustion. William Fernie quoted in his *Herbal Simples*:

To enliven the sad with the joy of a joke,
Give them wine with some borage put in to soak.

Simple: Infuse 1 oz of dried leaves in 1 pint of boiling water for 15 minutes. Strain and flavor with honey. Or 1 teaspoon of fresh herb to a cup of boiling water. The flowers frozen into ice cubes can be added to iced water and summer drinks.

CAUTION: DO NOT take if you are on the following medications: carbamazepine (Tegretol), phenobarbital, phenytoin (Dilantin), rifampin, rifabutin (Mycobutin), aspirin, clopidogrel (Plavix), diclofenac (Voltaren, Cataflam, others), ibuprofen (Advil, Motrin, others), naproxen (Anaprox, Naprosyn, others), dalteparin (Fragmin), enoxaparin (Lovenox), heparin, warfarin (Coumadin), ibuprofen (Advil, Motrin, Nuprin, others), indomethacin (Indocin), naproxen (Aleve, Anaprox, Naprelan, Naprosyn), and piroxicam (Feldene), as these drugs may cause potentially nasty side effects when combined with borage. If you are expecting to undergo surgery, you should stop taking borage at least two weeks before as it may interact with the anaesthetic.

Magical use: *Borage* flowers in the house help bring about domestic tranquility. Use an infusion spray to enhance peace and harmony.

Superstition and folklore: Valued in ancient times for its ability to dispel melancholy and impart courage, the flowers were included in stirrup cups offered to Crusaders departing for the Holy Land.

Personal Note: According to Dioscorides and Pliny, borage was the famous *nepenthe* of Homer, which when drunk steeped in wine, brought absolute forgetfulness. John Evelyn, writing at the close of the seventeenth-century tells us: *'Sprigs of Borage are of known virtue to revive the hypochondriac and cheer the hard student'*.

BOX

Scientific Name(s): *Buxus sempervirens*
Common Name(s): Boxwood;

Although all parts of the shrub are poisonous in times past it *was* used medicinally. Pliny recommended the berries for diarrhea but the repercussions were probably far longer reaching than a quick cure! It is better known for its use as hedging, topiary work and to shelter more tender plants. A close-clipped variety was used to make decorative edging to formal herb gardens. Box, like other somber evergreen, has long been a plant of grave decorations and funerals. Wordsworth describes a north-country funeral custom of filling a basin with sprigs of box and placing it by the door of the house from which the coffin was taken. Each person who attended the funeral would take a piece of box and throw it into the grave after the coffin had been lowered.

Simple: None.
Magical use: Sprigs of box can be used in place of the brush as an aspergillum to sprinkle consecrated water.
Superstition and folklore: There is evidence that some peculiar significance or virtue was once associated with the *box* by the discovery of twigs of this tree in the old burial mounds in Essex.
Personal Note: The leaves were formerly used in place of quinine, and as a fever reducer.

BRIAR (see Rose and Rosehips)

Scientific Name(s): *Rosa canina*
Common Name(s): Dog rose; wild rose;

Fossilised roses, dating back thousands of years, have been discovered throughout Europe, including Britain. In medieval times rose hips, rich in vitamin C, were made into syrup for cough medicines or by itself it was taken as a gentle tonic; the leaves were used as a mild laxative and, being astringent, for healing wounds. Rose water made a soothing antiseptic tonic for sore and sensitive skins while many other uses were found for the petals and hips in the kitchen. The plant can be found growing in the wild but can also be trained up a trellis in the garden. An old riddle – the five brethren of the rose – gives an effective way of identifying roses of the *canina* group and has been passed on orally since medieval times:

> *On a summer' day, in sultry weather,*
> *Five brethren were born together.*
> *Two had breads and two and none*
> *And the other had but half a one.*

The 'brethren' are the five sepals of the dog-rose, two of which are whiskered on both sides, two quite smooth and the fifth whiskered on one side only.

Simple: Wild rose petal tea may help good bacteria to grow in your digestive tract and has been used as an herbal remedy for constipation and diarrhoea. Rose petal tea may help prevent urinary tract infections due to its detox and diuretic properties.

Magical use: Roses are steeped in magical energy: they have protective powers as well as being used in charms for romance.

Superstition and folklore: The name 'dog rose' is said to have originated in ancient Greece, where the root was reputed to cure the bite from a rabid dog.

Personal Note: It seems the further north the dog rose grows, the richer the hips are in vitamin C; hence the content of those in Scotland is four times greater than those in southern England.

BROAD BEANS

Scientific Name(s): *Vicia faba*
Common Name(s): fava, butter, Windsor, horse or even English beans;

Archaeological evidence suggests that it was one of the first foods cultivated by man; their hardiness and ability to endure cold climates contributed to their endurance as a crop. It remained an important part of the diet throughout the Middle Ages, being able to be dried for storage over long periods, until it was superseded by the potato in the 16th century. Nutritionally, it is a good source of vitamins A and C, as well as potassium and iron. Young, fresh broad beans should be tender enough to be shelled and eaten, but mature beans develop a skin that must be removed. If they're young and tender, just steam for about three minutes; if they're a bit older, boiling is best as it softens and tenderises the skin - add to salads, risotto and pasta dishes, or eat as a side dish.

Simple: Rubbing a wart with a furry inside of a bean pod and then in great secrecy bury it; as the pod rots away in the ground, so was the wart subsides.

Magical use: Use beans to appease the spirits of the dead. Throw some around the outside of the home if a ghost or poltergeist is causing concern. Beans inspire creativity and communication and can be carried raw in a pouch or cooked and eaten for inspiration.

Superstition and folklore: Romans believed that the souls of their ancestors resided in fava *beans*. ... Since the *beans* were believed to hold souls they were thrown out as a decoy in hopes that the soul-hungry ghosts would be get confused and be sated with the *beans* and leave the family alone.

Personal Note: When planting it is wise to sow four beans in a row: 'One for the pigeon, one for the crow, one will wither and one will grow'.

BROOM

Scientific Name(s): *Sarothamnus sciparius; Cytisus sciparius; Planta genita*
Common Name(s): Plantagenita; Scotch broom;

Broom was used in ancient Anglo-Saxon medicine and by the Welsh physicians of the early Middle Ages. It had a place in the *London Pharmacopceia* of 1618 and is included in the *British Pharmacopoeia* of the present day. Culpeper recommended the plant for *'dropsy, gout, sciatica and pains of the hips and joints'* ... and its branches being used to make brooms. The flowers and buds were pickled and used for flavouring savoury snacks; also used for making an unguent to cure the gout and Henry VIII used to drink a water made from the flowers against this complaint. Apart from its use in heraldry, the broom has been associated with several popular traditions. In some parts, it used to be considered a sign of plenty, when it bore many flowers. The flowering tops were used for house decoration at the Whitsuntide festival but it was considered unlucky to employ them for menial purposes when in full bloom. An old Suffolk tradition runs:

If you sweep the house with blossomed Broom in May
You are sure to sweep the head of the house away.

It is essential that true broom be carefully distinguished from Spanish broom (*Spartium junceum*), since a number of cases of poisoning have occurred from the substitution of the dried flowers of *Spartium* for those of the true broom [*A Modern Herbal*].

Simple: Infusion of broom (*Infusum Scoparii*) is made by infusing the dried tops with boiling water for fifteen minutes and then straining. It was introduced in the *British Pharmacopoeia* of 1898, in place of the decoction of broom of the preceding issues. The infusion is made from 1oz of the dried tops to a pint of boiling water; taken in wineglassful doses frequently to increase the amount of water and salt expelled from the body as urine.

Magical use: Broom is used in spells for purification and protection.

Superstition and folklore: Geoffrey Plantagenet wore a sprig of broom (*Planta genista*) in his hat – hence it being adopted as the badge of the Plantagenet kings of England.

Personal Note: During the months of May and June, this deciduous shrub announces the arrival of summer by producing golden, almond-scented spikes of pea-flowers on wiry branches.

BRYONY

Scientific Name(s): *Bryonia dioica*
Common Name(s): Wild bryony; wild vine; tetterbury;

Although poisonous, bryony has been valued medicinally since ancient times. Culpeper warned that *'the root of bryony purges the belly with great violence, troubling the stomach and burning the liver, and therefore not rashly to be taken'*. Listed by Aelfric, the plant was cultivated in physic gardens and the roots were often sold as 'English mandrake' because the genuine root was so rare. English hedgerows exhibit bryony of two distinct sorts - the white and the black - which differ much, the one from the other, as to medicinal properties, and which belong to separate orders of plants.

Simple: None.

Magical use: In France, the white bryony is deemed so potent and perilous, that its root is named the devil's turnip - *navet du diable*.

Superstition and folklore: The bryony is an example of the strange phenomenon in plant lore, that of gender pairing, in which unrelated plants are paired as 'male' and 'female'. White bryony was regarded as female, black bryony as male. And so, traditionally, any remedy prepared would have to take this into account. The male of a pair could only treat a woman, and vice versa. [*Hatfield's Herbal*]

Personal Note: In medieval times the juice, mixed with deadly nightshade (*Atropa belladonna*), was used as an anaesthetic!

BURDOCK

Scientific Name(s) *Arctium minus*

Common Name(s): Sticky buttons; beggar's buttons;

Burdock root has been used for thousands of years for numerous medicinal uses, including purifying the blood and enhancing the lymphatic system. The first use of burdock is recorded in the medieval period, but there are some older records in Chinese herbal medicine. Over the years, there have been many ways on how to prepare the plant for consumption as either food or herbal medicine. Today, burdock still plays a significant role in terms of herbal remedies. Better yet, tea made from this herb is delicious and nutritious and is caffeine-free. While most herbs can be hard to find and expensive to obtain, burdock is easily cultivated as a wonderful vegetable and herb due to its numerous health benefits. Although all parts of this plant are edible, the root is the most beneficial hence the name burdock root.

Simple: Drinking tea from this herb helps detoxify the liver, cleanse the blood, and balance hormones, among other benefits; historically, burdock root was used to treat arthritis, colds, measles, sore throats and tonsillitis. Burdock tea is available in bags or as loose dried leaves and be bought in most local health shops and online stores. Place one tablespoon in a teacup and add the boiling water; let it steep for at least 5 minutes, then strain the loose leaves and enjoy Add honey or lemon juice to taste. For fresh root, use one that is firm and not too soft. Coarsely chop about 2 tablespoons of the root and place into a small stainless pot; add 3 cups of spring water and bring to a boil, then lower heat to simmer for 30 minutes. Allow to steep for another 20 minutes. Serve hot. Drink throughout the day as a detox tea. Remember, as with many herbal teas, burdock root tea is diuretic, so don't over-consume.

DANGER: DO NOT take if you are on anticoagulants, as burdock and anticoagulants can react with each other causing slow clotting and, in some cases, haemorrhage.

Magical use: The plant was believed to guard people against evil and negative energies.

Superstition and folklore: If you chance to get *burdocks* fastened into your clothes, it is a sign that you will have difficulty in your favorite undertaking. [*Encyclopædia of Superstitions, Folklore, and the Occult Sciences of the World*]

Personal Note: Dandelion and burdock is a beverage consumed in the British Isles since the Middle Ages. It was originally a type of light mead but over the years has evolved into the carbonated soft drink commercially available today – and was all part of childhood summer picnics.

BUTTERCUP

Scientific Name(s): *Ranunculus acris*
Common Name(s): Goldweed; Soldier Buttons; kingcup; crowpeckle; beggar's weed;

According to *Country Seasons*, the '*buttercup comes into flower at the very peak of Spring to spark water meadows and rough pasture land with a profusion of golden bloom and fretted green leaf'*. Despite its nursery connection of 'buttercups and daisies', however, the plant is poisonous and will cause blisters should the foliage remain in contact with the skin for any length of time. These inflammations can take a long time to heal and Culpeper described the plant as *'this furious biting herb'*. Beggars used buttercup poultices to inflict their own skin with sores and so the plant was also known as Lararus or beggar's weed. Fernie refers to the plant in his *Herbal Simples* as a treatment for various complaints but it is not to be recommended as the sap from fresh stems will blister the skin.

Simple: None.

Magical use: For protection, hang a bunch of the flowers over the front door.

Superstition and folklore: People held a fresh buttercup flower under the chin of a friend or family member. If a yellow reflection from the flower's shiny petals can be seen under the chin, the person is said to 'like butter'. This custom is still taught to young children and shows how buttercup petals reflect light and attract pollinators.

Personal note: Buttercups are frequently featured in medieval church carvings

CABBAGE

Scientific Name(s): *Brassica oleracea*
Common Name(s): Wild cabbage;

The inexpensiveness and health benefits of cabbage earned it its nickname 'drug of the poor' during the Middle Ages; while many modern studies have suggested that increasing consumption of plant-based foods like cabbage decreases the risk of diabetes, obesity, cancer and heart disease. It can also help promote a healthy complexion, increased energy, and overall lower weight. Cabbage is great for our health due to its impressive nutritional profile. It comes in different shapes and colors (red, purple, white and green) with either crinkled or smooth leaves.

Apart from being a part of many delicious dishes, it also is an ingredient for many home remedies.

- Cabbage is used in to remove pus from ingrown toenails and eliminate the infection. Place several leaves around the infected toe and secure with a cloth bandage; cover with a sock and leave overnight. Remove the leaves in the morning and soak the infected toe in an Epsom salt bath for 10-15 minutes. Repeat the process overnight and continue for a few days to see a vast improvement.
- Cabbage helps in alleviating pain, and also reduces swelling of the feet. Cool large white or green cabbage leaves in the freezer until they are chilled. Wrap them around the swollen foot and sit with foot elevated for 30 minutes. The cabbage will draw out excess fluid and bring relief to sore feet.
- Cabbage water is said to be good for the skin because of its vitamin E, does, indeed, stimulate the digestive system, and is even a hangover aid because of its vitamin C content, which also boosts the immune system. A cup of hot, strained cabbage water helps keep the digestive tract free from disease and infection.

Simple: The leaves of a cabbage turned to a puree in a blender to produce a face mask that is a good treatment for teenage facial spots. Apply evenly to the clean skin of the face and leave for 15-20 minutes and wash off. Keep in the fridge overnight and repeat the following day, or for as long as necessary.

Magical use: Used in spells to draw good luck.

Superstitions and folklore: *The Farmer's Almanac* tells us of various American folklore elements that say eating cabbage on New Year's Day will attract a financial windfall. Many of these customs would have arrived in the US with Old World immigrants.

Personal note: According to physician William Alcott:

Lettuce, greens and celery, though much eaten, are worse than cabbage, being equally indigestible without the addition of condiments. Besides, the lettuce contains narcotic properties. It is said of Galen, that he used to obtain from a head of it, eaten on going to bed, all the good effects of a dose of opium.

CALENDULA

Scientific Name(s): *Calendula officinalis*
Common Name(s): Pot marigold; ruddes;

Calendula is a freely re-seeding annual that blooms all season long and makes a lovely addition to gardens with full sun. This is a centuries-old antifungal, antiseptic, wound-healing herb. The petals of these cheerful yellow-and-orange daisy-like flowers lend skin-soothing properties to many natural cosmetics. Harvest the petals fresh in the morning after the dew has dried, or dry entire blooms - which close in the evening - before they form seeds. The petals are edible and can be used fresh in salads or dried and used to colour cheese or as a replacement for saffron.

Simple: As a lotion for bathing cuts and abrasions, and as a mouthwash or gargle for mouth ulcers, sore gums and throat infections, infuse 1 teaspoon dried flowers and leaves in 1 cup of boiling water. A compress or poultice using marigold is an excellent first aid treatment for burns, scalds and stings.
CAUTION: DO NOT take calendula if you are on the following medications: clonazepam (Klonopin), lorazepam (Ativan), phenobarbital (Donnatal), zolpidem (Ambien) as it can cause excessive sleepiness when mixed with these drugs.
Magical use: Includes prophesy, legal matters, psychic energy and renewing personal energy.
Superstition and folklore: The flowers are open when the sun is out. The marigold is also called the 'herb of the sun', representing passion and even creativity. It was also said to be highly effective

for allaying gossip.

Personal note: The ancient Romans named this plant *calendula* because they noticed that it was blooming on the first day of every month (*calends*). It was a *symbol* of joy and happiness in their gardens, and because it provided them with a continuous supply of *flowers* and tender leaves, it was used regularly for cooking and in medicine.

CARROT

Scientific name(s): *Daucus carota*
Common name(s): Wild carrot;

Wild carrots, listed by Aelfric, are still found in the hedgerows of Britain. Although carrots were eaten as a vegetable by the Greeks and Romans, they were not cultivated in Britain until medieval times. Eating them was traditionally claimed to be good for the eyes, especially for the improvement of night vision. **Carrots** are vegetables that have a healthy taste and qualities, being known for their high content of carotene, which is converted in the body into vitamin A. Besides carotene, carrots contain many vitamins - B1, B2, B6, C, D, E, K and PP, as well as many useful minerals and enzymes, and some essential oils.

Simple: Carrots are used in vitamin deficiency, anemia, colds and upset stomachs; useful in diseases of the heart and blood vessels as well as kidney stones. **Carotene** is absorbed better by the body if it is combined with fat, because it is fat soluble. That's why carrots should be eaten with butter, olive oil, cream or other fats as a cooked vegetable, raw in salads or as a snack.

Magical use: *Carrot juice is u*sed by men to encourage a deep connection with the sensual and sexual self. Helps ground excess energy.

Superstition and folklore: Eating carrots was said to help a person see in the dark, which might be due to a myth begun by the Air Ministry in World War II. To prevent the Germans finding out that Britain was using radar to intercept bombers on night raids, they issued press releases stating that British pilots were eating lots of carrots to give them exceptional night vision. They did such an excellent job keeping a straight face (and supporting their lie with propaganda posters and supporting documents) that the idea carrots improve vision (especially night vision) remains firmly embedded in popular lore over half a century later.

Personal note: Botanists have argued that medieval carrots were purple, or almost black, yet an illustration in the 12th-centurt herbal of Bury St Edmunds depicts the vegetable with an orange root.

CENTAURY

Scientific Name(s): *Centaureum erythraea*
Common Name(s): Centaury Gentian; Red Centaury; filwort; Christ's Ladder; feverwort;

Centaury is used as a medical herb in many parts of Europe. The herb, mainly prepared as tea, is said to be beneficial for patients with gastric and complaints of the liver. We also find a reference to it in *Le Petit Albert*: '

Fifteen magical herbs of the Ancients are given … The eleventh hearbe is named of the Chaldees, Isiphon . . . of Englishmen, Centory . . . this herbe hath a marvellous virtue, for if it be joined with the blood of a female lapwing, or black plover, and put with oile in a lamp, all that compass it about shall believe themselves to be witches, so that one shall believe of another that his head is in heaven and his feete on earth; and if the aforesaid thynge be put in the fire when the starres shine it shall appeare yt the sterres runne one agaynste another and fyghte.' [English translation, 1619]

Simple: The dried herb is given in infusions of 1 oz of the dried herb to 1 pint of water, and used extensively in dyspepsia, for languid digestion with heartburn after food. When run down and suffering from want of appetite, centaury tea - taken three or four times daily, half an hour before meals, is found of great benefit. [*A Modern Herbal*]

Magical use: Also, in a translation of an old mediaeval Latin poem of the tenth century, by Macer, there is mention of centaury (with other herbs) as being powerful against 'wykked sperytis'.

Superstition and folklore: In Lucan's *Pharsalia*, *centaury* is one of the plants named as being burned with the object of driving away serpents.

Personal note: Said to have been named after Chiron the centaur of Greek mythology, who used the herb to heal himself of a wound contaminated by the blood of the many-headed serpent Hydra.

CHAMOMILE

Scientific Name(s): *Chamomilla recutita*
Common Name(s): Manzanilla;

Chamomile was a great favourite of the Anglo-Saxon herbals and in the 16th-century was used as a perfumed ground cover for paths in the gardens of large houses. Infusions are good for easing tension, headaches and irritability, especially where associated with digestive problems. Fernie recommends that chamomile tea is *'an excellent drink for aged persons to be taken before dinner'*. Chamomile is also one of the most versatile herbs for external use as it reduces inflammation and promotes tissue healing. For convenience it is available in teabag form from all good heath shops.

Simple: Infuse 1 oz dried blossoms for 15 minutes in 1 pint boiling water; for a single cup, infuse 1 teaspoon flowers in 1 cup boiling water. Strain and flavour with honey if required. *As the value of chamomile rests chiefly in its volatile essential oil, always make sure the container used for making the infusion is covered while in use; when making a single cup, cover the cup with a saucer'.* [*Mastering Herbalism*]

Magical use: A herb of purification and protection, and can be used in incenses for sleep and meditation. Plant it around your home to ward against psychic or magical attack.

Superstition and folklore: According to *The Modern Herbal*: *'When walked on, its strong, fragrant scent will often reveal its presence before it is seen'.* For this reason, it was employed as one of the aromatic strewing herbs in the Middle Ages, and used often to be purposely planted in green walks in gardens. Indeed, walking over the plant seems especially beneficial to it.

Like a camomile bed
The more it is trodden
The more it will spread

Personal note: The aromatic fragrance gives no hint of its bitterness of taste.

CHERVIL

Scientific Name(s): *Anthriscus cerefolium*
Common Name(s): French parsley; sweet Cicely;

A native of the Middle East and eastern and southern Europe, the herb was almost certainly introduced into Britain by the Romans as it was listed by Aelfric. It was valued as a cleansing tonic, especially for the liver, kidneys and stomach. Applied externally as a warm poultice, the leaves relieved aching joints, swellings and haemorrhoids. The leaves eaten raw stimulated digestion. As a Lenten (or Mary Garden) herb, chervil was traditionally taken for its restorative and blood-cleansing properties. In various folk medicines, it was used as eyewash to refresh the eyes and ingested as tea to reduce blood pressure.

Simple: Chervil tea is easy to make: put a handful of fresh herbs (about ¼ cup) per cup of tea into a pot. Pour boiling water over the herbs, cover, and steep for three to five minutes.

Magical use: In modern times this *plant* is known as a pot *herb* in our gardens but it can be helpful for purification and protection purposes if infused as a room spray.

Superstition and folklore: Slugs are attracted to chervil and the plant is sometimes used to bait them

Personal note: It is commonly used to season mild-flavoured dishes and is a constituent of the French herb mixture *fines herbes*.

CHICKWEED

Scientific Name(s): *Stellaria media*
Common Name(s): Common wintergreen;

In the dark month of January there is little available by way of 'wild food' for use in our country kitchen. If the frost hasn't been too severe, we may be lucky enough to find a supply of early chickweed in the garden or field edge. This common weed can be cooked with spring onions as a fresh vegetable (cook for 2 mins with a knob of butter), and is one of the tenderest of wild green stuff. Witches are probably more familiar with it as a healing and soothing agent, made into a decoction to wash and bathe swollen and inflamed injuries. It's been used in this way for centuries in domestic plant medicine, being listed by Nicholas Culpeper for relieving itching skin conditions. Sailors used chickweed vinegar to prevent scurvy when fresh citrus was unavailable.

Simple: It has been used since forever as a poultice for skin conditions, boils and insect bites.

Magical use: The tiny white flower has ten petals and can be used in spells of protection and when we look at the chickweed itself, close up we can see that the petals themselves are paired and shoot off in five rays. The sepals (the small leaves right behind the petals) form a pentagram. The pistil (the female organs of a flower) is shaped almost like *triskele* - Celtic symbol for the motion of action, cycles, progress, revolution and competition. So much magical symbolism is present in this tiny, unassuming little flower.

Superstition and folklore: Lord Bacon wrote that when the *chickweed* expands its leaves fully and boldly, no rain will fall for twenty-four hours.

Personal note: I usually have a plentiful supply growing in an old wheelbarrow but the wild birds have helped themselves – and they're welcome to it. The only other plentiful supply is on the neighbour's muck heap but I don't fancy that – and, obviously, neither do the birds!

CINQUEFOIL

Scientific Name(s): *Potentilla anserine*
Common Name(s): Creeping tormentil; silverweed;

From prehistoric times until the introduction of the potato in the 16th century, the starchy roots of the plant were eaten raw, or cooked and ground to make porridge and bread. In medieval times it was applied externally to cuts and wound, or used as a gargle for sore throats and mouth ulcers.

Simple: Use one to two tablespoonfuls of chopped fresh cinquefoil root and boil it in a pint of water. Allow to steep for twenty minutes before straining and cooling. The lukewarm herbal infusion can be made into a moist compress and applied to the affected areas of the body.

Magical use: Cinquefoil's five leaves are said to stand for love, money, health, power, and wisdom. Carry some in a sachet or small bottle to possess these qualities.

Superstition and folklore: Reputedly used by Roman soldiers on long marches to relieve the soreness of the feet and later placed in the shoes of pilgrims.

Personal note: It was also said that medieval fishermen would attach the plant to their nets to increase their catch.

CLEAVERS

Scientific Name(s): *Galium aparine*
Common Name(s): Sticky Willie; sticky Jack; goose grass;

Cleavers was once used as a potherb. It was a useful plant in medieval kitchens because it could be picked in frost or snow. The plant's hook-like bristles soften when boiled and its chopped leaves and stem can be made into soups and stews; the tender shoots can be boiled and buttered as a vegetable. Medicinally, cleavers is calming to skin irritations, having an astringent and antiseptic action making this herb good for healing wounds. It will reduce inflammation, detoxify and cleanse the skin so can be used to treat eczema, dermatitis, and psoriasis, as well as boils and abscesses.

Simple: An infusion may be made by steeping 1½ oz of the chopped herb in a pint of warm water for 2 hours and used as a lotion or compress direct to the skin when cold.

Magic use: In traditional magic potions and rituals for protective properties and its tenacious nature.

Superstition and folklore: A cleavers protective knot bound with hand spun red cord hung over the doorway of a home invokes a loving atmosphere around all those that pass under it.

Personal note: Herdsmen from ancient Greece onwards used bundles of cleavers for filtering animal hairs out of milk.

CLOVE-PINK

Scientific Name(s): *Dianthus caryophyllus*
Common Name(s): Gilly flower;

Clove pinks were grown in monastic gardens mainly for their beauty and fragrance. Used as a nerve tonic in the past, today carnation is grown commercially in France for its rich clove-like essential oil that is used in perfumery. Clove Pink is the wild ancestor of today's garden carnation which has been developed into cultivars of different colours. Fresh petals, with the bitter white base removed, can be candied, pickled in vinegar, added to salads and be used to flavor fruit.

Simple: Pick the flowers in the morning on a warm, sunny day and separate the blossoms from the green calyx by pulling gently on the petals. Pack the petals into a measuring jug and determine how much syrup to make by using a proportion of 2/3 cup flours to 1 cup of syrup. To make the syrup use 1 part water to 1 part sugar and boil it for 5 minutes. Take the syrup off the heat and stir in the flowers. Cover the pot and put aside to infuse overnight. Filter the flowers out of the syrup into a glass jar and keep the syrup covered in a cool but not cold place. Use it within 3-4 days or until it looks or smells doubtful. Other than just smelling it for a heady shot of aromatherapy, a tablespoon or two in a glass of warm water is a sweet and fragrant beverage for hot summer days.

Magical use: *Clove pink* petals are also wonderful for strewing in a *magical* context and the flower's *clove*-like scent is helpful in trance and astral work.

Superstition and folklore: In medieval art the flower was a symbol of betrothal and floated in the drinks of the engaged couple.

Personal note: *Malmaison* is one of the most famous fragrances of the old English house of Floris (founded in 1730).

CLOVER

Scientific Name(s): *Trifolium repens*
Common Name(s): White or red clover; trefoil;

Pliny said that when clover leaves trembled and stood upright a storm or tempest was on its way. During medieval times the flowers were valued by bee-keepers, because their nectar made superior honey. Modern scientific tests have shown that **red clover** contains isoflavones, plant-based chemicals that produce estrogen-like effects in the body. The flower heads of **white clover** were used as blood cleanser, to clean wounds sores, boils and heal eye ailments.

Simple: Clover infusion made from **white clover** blossoms can be used as an eyewash. **Red clover** can be infused in hot water to make a delicious herbal tea. To make, pour hot water over 1-3 teaspoons of red clover, and let steep for 10-15 minutes. This tea has a natural light sweetness to it, but add honey if desired. Because the flowers are edible, they can also be used to brighten up a salad.

DANGER: Taking large amounts of clover may damage your liver and cause clotting problems. If you are regularly taking any of the following drugs, do not take clover: Paracetamol (acetaminophen Tylenol and others), amiodarone (Cordarone), carbamazepine (Tegretol), isoniazid (INH), methotrexate (Rheumatrex), methyldopa (Aldomet), fluconazole (Diflucan), itraconazole (Sporanox), erythromycin (Erythrocin, Ilosone, others), phenytoin (Dilantin), lovastatin (Mevacor), pravastatin (Pravachol), simvastatin (Zocor), aspirin, clopidogrel (Plavix), diclofenac (Voltaren, Cataflam, others), ibuprofen (Advil, Motrin, others), naproxen (Anaprox, Naprosyn, others), dalteparin (Fragmin), enoxaparin (Lovenox), heparin, and warfarin (Coumadin).

Magical use: The leaves were worn to bring good luck; and to protect against evil and witchcraft. The rare four-leafed clover was considered especially lucky (provided it wasn't given away) and was reputed to bestow on its owner clairvoyant powers.

Superstition and folklore: The luck of the four-leaf clover is the most identifiable clover superstition but is only a small piece of clover-lore. Clovers are versatile plants capable of bringing you a spouse, healing your ailments, or driving away evil spirits. Depending on the variety and number of leaves, the superstitions surrounding clover can vary widely.

Personal note: Keep a few patches of uncut clover because the bees love it – and clover honey is generally milder in flavor that wildflower honey.

COLTSFOOT

Scientific Name(s): *Tussilag farfara*
Common Name(s): Coughwort; hallfoot; horsehoof; ass's foot; foalswort; fieldhove; bullsfoot; donnhove;

An old name for Coltsfoot was *Filius ante patrem* ('the son before the father'), because the star-like, golden flowers appear and wither before the broad, sea-green leaves are produced. Hot or cold, coltsfoot tea compresses can be applied to swollen areas, and a cool compress is soothing on the forehead or stomach when one has a fever. A poultice of the leaves or flowers can be applied to eczema, sores, ulcers and insect bites.

Simple: A decoction is made of 1 oz of leaves, in 1 quart of water boiled down to a pint, sweetened with honey and taken in teacupful doses for coughs, colds and asthma.

CAUTION: DO NOT take coltsfoot if you suffer from high blood pressure. May also cause the following medications to stop working correctly: carbamazepine (Tegretol), phenobarbital, phenytoin (Dilantin), rifampin, rifabutin (Mycobutin), aspirin, clopidogrel (Plavix), diclofenac (Voltaren, Cataflam, others), ibuprofen (Advil, Motrin, others), naproxen (Anaprox, Naprosyn, others), dalteparin (Fragmin), enoxaparin (Lovenox), heparin, and warfarin (Coumadin).

Magical use: As a *magical* herb it is considered to increase psychic awareness and is generally mixed with other so-called 'psychic herbs' for greater effect ...

Superstition and folklore: In the language of flowers, this flower signifies: 'Justice shall be done' [*Encyclopaedia of Superstitions*]

Personal note: In Paris, the coltsfoot flowers used to be painted as a sign on the doorpost of an apothecary's shop.

COMFREY (dwarf)
Scientific Name(s): *Symphytum grandiflorum*
Common Name(s): Knitbone; bruisewort;

Comfrey has been cultivated for healing since 400 BC when it was used by such notable Greek physicians as Herodotus, Nicander, Galen, and Dioscorides. It continued to be used throughout history and its use spread through Europe since dwarf and wild comfrey share the same healing properties. *Dwarf comfrey* is a native herb in Britain and as the name suggests, this is a shorter variety reaching only 12 inches high but it will spread up to three feet across. It has a myriad of uses, and *comfrey* is one of the most useful plants you can grow in your garden. Buds are pink to red, flowers are bluish-white with blue base, creating a tri-colour effect. Common comfrey's (*symphytum offcinale*) original name, knitbone, derives from the external use of poultices of its leaves and roots to heal burns, sprains, swelling, and bruises.

Comfrey can also be used to create a powerful liquid fertiliser, as well as a compost activator to produce enriched compost. It can create a fertiliser base within the soil, as well as a nutritious mulch on top. You can also use the dead leaves to make leaf mould as a nutritious potting compost and a 'tea' which will be of benefit to the tomato plants, and all fruiting vegetables in the garden (e.g., pumpkins, courgettes, squash). The basic idea of making a comfrey tea is to harvest the leaves and soak them in water for about a month. This potassium-rich liquid is then applied as a feed to fruiting plants. Mature comfrey plants can be harvested 3-4 times each year as it grows back quickly and can be cut again about a month later.

Simple: To make a comfrey compress, gather a half dozen large comfrey leaves and roughly cut them into 2-inch pieces (including stems.) Place pieces in either food processor or blender, along with ½ cup of water. Purée/pulse on 'high' until liquid; spread on a piece of clean linen and leave on for 10-15 minutes. Comfrey is excellent applied to shallow wounds, poorly healing skin, strains, sprains and fractures, but should not be used for deep wounds as the surface can heal over too rapidly which may lead to abscesses.

CAUTION: Comfrey should not be used during pregnancy and lactation, by infants, and in people with liver, kidney, or vascular diseases.

Magical use: Comfrey is used in protective magic. It is also used in many travel amulets to keep travelers safe and alert. Because comfrey has many 'grounding' properties it can be used in any herbal blend to strengthen energy shields and protect the home, business or automobile from theft or intrusion.

Superstition and folklore: From the Highlands of Scotland to south-west England comfrey has been used in British folk medicine for treating sprains and fractures - a magical herb of folklore, was once thought to cure the ailments of man or beast.

Personal note: Although it is listed as being native to Britain, the plant was said to have been brought to England by Crusaders returning from the Holy Land, with some varieties being brought from Russia in the 1800s.

CORNFLOWER

Scientific Name(s): *Centaurea cyanus*
Common Name(s): Bluebottle; hurt-sickle; bachelor's buttons;

In medieval times an infusion of cornflowers was used for digestive and gastric disorders and the flowers used to produce a lotion for sore and tired eyes. The petals were used fresh in salads. Culpeper wrote that *'the juice pit into fresh or green wounds doth quickly solder up the lips of them together ...'* He also suggested that the country name of hurt-sickle was because the tough stems blunted the edges of the sickles that reap the corn. The plant's medicinal value lies primarily in its anti-inflammatory properties. Taken internally as a tea, the flowers can also impart their antibiotic and antioxidant properties as a preventative for warding off illnesses like the common cold.

Simple: To make an herbal infusion of the flower heads for use as an eyewash, take two teaspoons of the dried petals and add to a steaming cup of water. Allow to cool and then strain the infusion before using as a refreshing wash for tired eyes or splashing on irritated skin. To make cornflower tea, place a teaspoon of the dried herbs in a cup of boiling water. Let the mix stand for about 5-7 minutes then drink.

Magical use: In ancient Egypt, cornflowers were associated with renewal or revival, as they appeared each year growing amidst cereal crops like wheat and barley.

Superstition and folklore: Also known as 'bachelor's buttons', a general legend states the flower was worn by young men in love and if the flower faded too quickly it meant that the young lady didn't return his affections.

Personal note: The cornflower is a national symbol of Estonia but the flower was a folk emblem for many years prior to that. Blue cornflowers are part of the traditional garlands young Estonian girls wear for festivals, and the cornflower is regularly used as a motif in local folk art.

COWSLIP

Scientific Name(s): *Primula verts*
Common Name(s): Bunch of keys' paigles; Herb Peter;

Commenting on the herb's reputation as a wrinkle-removing cosmetic, Culpeper wrote that *'our city dames know well enough the ointment or distilled water of it adds to beauty, or at least restores it when it is lost'*. Cowslip leaves were used as a salve for healing wounds, and the flowers as a mild sedative. Cowslip tea was recommended for headaches, insomnia and nervous tension. The leaves and flowers were eaten in salads. The flowers were used to make cowslip wine right up to the mid-20th-century; they were also crystallized or sugared.

Simple: Cowslips contain flavonoids in the flowers and is astringent throughout; an infusion can be taken to relieve headaches and insomnia. A tea of cowslip flowers is made from a spoonful of dried flowers over which a cup of boiling water is poured; it is then left to infuse for 10 minutes after which it is consumed.

Magical use: Old myths claimed that fairies sought refuge inside cowslips in times of danger and this was reflected in Ariel's song from the *Tempest* ... *In a cowslips bell I lie / There I couch when owls do cry* ...

Superstition and folklore: The name is thought to derive from the Old English for cow dung or cowpat from which the plant was said to spring.

Personal note: This beautiful wild flower is not as abundant as once it was and needs protecting so it is best grown in the garden for harvesting.

DANDELION

Scientific Name(s): *Taraxacum officinale*
Common Name(s): Piss-abed;

Dandelion is possibly one of the most widely prescribed medicinal plant in Western herbalism. The leaf is traditionally used in spring as a cleansing infusion to treat water retention and rheumatism. The young leaves of the plant make an agreeable and wholesome addition to spring salads and are often eaten on the Continent, especially in France. The full-grown leaves should not be taken, being too bitter, but young leaves, especially if blanched, make an excellent salad, either alone or in combination with other plants, lettuce, shallot tops or chives. Young dandelion leaves make delicious sandwiches if laid between slices of bread and butter and sprinkled with salt. The addition of a little lemon-juice and pepper varies the taste. The leaves should always be torn to pieces, rather than cut, in order to preserve the flavour.

Simple: Dandelion tea can have many positive effects on our digestive system, while offering potential health *benefits*, such as reducing inflammation, improving cholesterol levels, and fighting flu. Place the dandelion leaves in the teacup and cover with boiling water, allowing the leaves to steep for 10 minutes. Strain and add honey if desired.

DANGER: DO NOT take dandelion if you are taking antibiotics or blood thinners as it reduces their action. **CAUTION:** Dandelion also reduces the effectiveness of the following medications: Lithium, amitriptyline (Elavil), haloperidol (Haldol), ondansetron (Zofran), propranolol (Inderal), theophylline (Theo-Dur, others), and verapamil (Calan, Isoptin, others).

Magical use: Bring the flowers into the home to dispel dark thoughts and negative energy. Some people use dandelions to enhance psychic abilities and in his *Encyclopedia of Magical Herbs,* author Scott Cunningham recommends dandelion tea to aid in divination and prophetic dreaming.

Superstition and folklore: Known by its country name that derives from the French word [for dandelion] is *pissenlit*, which translates to 'pee the bed'.

Personal Note: Since they provide essential spring food for bumble bees it is recommended that lawns be left uncut for a fortnight to give the flowers a chance to bloom.

DAISY

Scientific Name(s): *Bellis perennis*
Common Name(s): Bruisewort;

In medieval times daisies were mainly used in ointments to heal wounds and bruises; they were also prescribed for stiff necks, swellings, lumbago and all kinds of aches and pains. A symbol of mid-summer would be a posy of daisies that country girls would have made into a daisy-chain to wear in their hair for the celebration. For such a small flower, daisies have played a significant part in folklore over a long time and we can use either the common garden/meadow daisy or the larger ox- or dog-daisy that even Chaucer commented upon:

Of all the flowers in the meadow,
I love these red and white flowers the most,
Such as men call daisies in our town,
For them, I have great affection,
When May comes, Before dawn,
I am up and walking in the meadow,
To see this flower again
That blissful sight chases away all my sorrow.

Simple: People take wild daisy tea for coughs, bronchitis, disorders of the liver and kidneys, and swelling (inflammation).

They also use it as a drying agent (astringent) and as a 'blood purifier'. [*eMedicineHealth*] To make a small pot of daisy tea, simply take a small handful of daisies with fairly short stalks, and steep in boiling water and wait for around 5-10 minutes.

Magical use: Used in folk-spells for health, wealth and happiness.

Superstition and folklore: An old proverb states that it isn't spring until you can plant your foot upon twelve daisies.

Personal Note: The botanical name *Bellis* may derive from the Latin for 'pretty', or from *bellum*, meaning 'war' – possibly a reference to its use on the battlefield as a wound herb.

DILL

Scientific Name(s): *Anethum graveolens* or *Peucedanum graveolens*
Common Name(s): Dillweed;

Dill is a hardy annual, a native of the Mediterranean region and Southern Russia. It grows wild among the corn in Spain and Portugal and upon the coast of Italy, but rarely occurs as a cornfield weed in Northern Europe. Dill seeds were used to make a cordial to relieve digestive problems, flatulence, stomach cramps, headaches and insomnia; while the leaves and seeds were used as flavourings for vinegars and cooked dished, particularly fish - and as a pickling spice for cucumbers and gherkins. Oil of Dill was used in mixtures, or administered in doses of 5 drops on lump sugar, but its most common use was in the preparation of 'dill water', which is a common domestic remedy for the flatulence of infants – i.e., gripe water. Although the herbal blend of anise, dill and fennel has been removed from the market in Ireland, mums are buying it online or getting it from the North and England where it is still on sale.

Simple: Use 2 teaspoons of bruised seeds per cup of hot water to make dill tea to soothe an upset stomach.

DANGER: Dill interferes with lithium and can increase how much lithium is in the body resulting in serious side effects. **DO NOT** take dill if you are taking lithium.

Magical use: In the Middle Ages, dill was one of the herbs used by magicians in their spells, and charms against witchcraft. In Drayton's *Nymphidia* are the lines: *Therewith her Vervain and her Dill / That hindereth Witches of their Will.*

Superstition and folklore: The herb was also added to love potions and witches' spells; or hung up in a house as protection against the 'evil eye'.

Personal Note: In medieval times the seeds were chewed to freshen the breath, and to allay hunger pains – especially during long church services!

DOCK

Scientific Name(s): *Rumex obtusifolius*
Common Name(s): Common dock; butter dock;

Both yellow and broad-leaved docks were used for the same medicinal purposes, notably to treat skin complaints, liver disorders and respiratory problems. The roots were used as a laxative, and for anaemia. The young leaves, although bitter, were cooked as a vegetable; Culpeper said they were *'as wholesome a pot herb as any growing in the garden'*.

Simple: The leaves are often applied externally as a rustic remedy in the treatment of blisters, burns and scalds. Dock leaves actually help relieve a nettle sting because rubbing vigorously releases moist sap from the leaves which has a cooling, soothing effect on the skin.

Magical use: Europeans used the seeds in money charms. They were soaked in water and the liquid was sprinkled throughout the shop to bring customers, according to Cunningham's encyclopedia of magical herbs.

Superstition and folklore: In country districts the leaves were used to wrap butter, hence the name 'butter-dock'.

Personal use: In country areas the leaves of the dock also provided impromptu toilet paper!

ELDER (Berry & Flower)

Scientific Name(s): *Sambucus nigra*

Common Name(s): Poor man's medicine chest; Elen wood;

Elder has a great number of folklore associations and has long been related to witchcraft and religion, which may partly reflect the wide range of medicinal uses of the different parts of the plant. Witches were said to be able to turn themselves into elder trees. Gypsies believe that it is very bad luck to cut down and/or burn elder wood as the Elder Mother will take revenge.

Simple: Got the sniffles? Elderflower tea is the answer! It has strong antioxidant properties and antiviral effect, which makes elderflower tea quite popular for fighting cold, flu and their symptoms. Brewing a cup of elderflower tea can also make a great mouthwash due to its flavor and antiviral properties. Use this tea for gargling as it will help soothe coughs, colds, hoarseness (laryngitis). Simple to prepare. You just need 1 teaspoon of dried elderflowers - put the dried flowers in a tea strainer and pour the hot water on top of them in a mug. Cover and steep for 10 minutes and enjoy!

DO NOT take if you are on immune suppressants as elderberry increases the immune system. If you are taking any of the following medications, do not take elderberry: azathioprine (Imuran), basiliximab (Simulect), cyclosporine (Neoral, Sandimmune), daclizumab (Zenapax), muromonab-CD3 (OKT3, Orthoclone OKT3), mycophenolate (CellCept), tacrolimus (FK506, Prograf), sirolimus (Rapamune), prednisone (Deltasone, Orasone), corticosteroids (glucocorticoids). **CAUTION: DO NOT** take elderflower if you are diabetic as it reduces the effect of diabetic medications, causing your blood sugar to drop too low.

Magical use: Growing an elder in your garden will protect your property from misfortune and harm.

Superstition and folklore: Cut down an elder tree and you could attract a lot of negative karma!

Personal Note: Burning elder wood in the hearth or need fire will attract misfortune.

FENNEL

Scientific Name(s) *Foeniculum vulgare*
Common Names: Sticky Jack; Sticky Willie;

The medieval herbalist Hildegarde of Bingen regarded fennel as an all-purpose herb that promoted good health. In mediaeval times, fennel was employed, together with St. John's Wort and other herbs, as a preventative of witchcraft and other evil influences. It was likewise eaten as a condiment to the salt fish so much consumed by our forefathers during Lent and to aid digestion. In Italy and France, the tender leaves are often used for garnishes and to add flavour to salads; also added, finely chopped, to sauces served with puddings. The tender stems are included in soups in Italy, though they are more frequently eaten raw as a salad. John Evelyn, in his *Acetaria* (1680), held that the peeled stalks, soft and white, of the cultivated garden fennel, when dressed like celery exercised a pleasant action conducive to sleep. The Italians eat these peeled stems, which they call *cartucci* as a salad, cutting them when the plant is about to bloom and serving with a dressing of vinegar and pepper. Fennel water has properties similar to those of anise and dill water: mixed with sodium bicarbonate and syrup, these waters constitute the domestic 'gripe water', used to correct the flatulence of infants.

Simple: The plant's chief use in herbal medicines today is as a gentle digestive stimulant. Infuse 1 teaspoon dried, bruised fennel seeds and leaves in ½ pint boiling water. Cover and let cool, then strain, and flavor as required before taking.

CAUTION: DO NOT take fennel if you are taking contraceptive drugs, Ciprofloxacin, conjugated equine estrogens (Premarin), Ethinyl estradiol, estradiol, tamoxifen (Nolvadex). Fennel decreases the effect of all these medications.

Magical use: Valued by the ancient Greeks and Romans, who believed it bestowed strength and courage; it was one of the nine herbs sacred to the Anglo-Saxons along with thyme, crabapple, nettle, mugwort, lamb's cress, betony, plantain, and chamomile

Superstition and folklore: Hung over doors or inserted in keyholes, fennel was reputed to ward off evil spirits.

Personal note: Old herbalists used fennel go improve memory and as an aphrodisiac.

FEVERFEW

Scientific Name(s): *Tanacetum parthenium*
Common Name(s): Feverfew; golden moss;

An age-old pain relief that has been in use since the Middle Ages, and later Culpeper recommended it for 'all pains in the head'; while current research has proven the efficacy of the plant in relieving the pain of migraine and headaches. Feverfew tea has long been a folk medicine for bringing down a fever and the leaves can be used either as fresh or dried for headaches. Alternatively, for migraine relief put one or two medium-sized leaves between two small slice of bread and eat them slowly when an attack is anticipated.

Simple: For headache relief place 1 teaspoon of leaves into a tea ball. Set the ball into a drinking cup and pour over boiling water; allow the tea to steep for five minutes and drink while it is still warm.

CAUTION: DO NOT take feverfew if you are on anticoagulants, antiplatelet drugs, or: amitriptyline (Elavil), haloperidol (Haldol), ondansetron (Zofran), propranolol (Inderal), theophylline (Theo-Dur, others), and verapamil (Calan, Isoptin, others) diclofenac (Cataflam, Voltaren), ibuprofen (Motrin), meloxicam (Mobic), piroxicam (Feldene), lovastatin (Mevacor), ketoconazole (Nizoral), itraconazole (Sporanox), fexofenadine (Allegra), triazolam (Halcion) and celecoxib (Celebrex). Feverfew inhibits the actions of all of these medications and interacts with GERD medications such as omeprazole (Prilosec), lansoprazole (Prevacid), and pantoprazole (Protonix); diazepam (Valium); carisoprodol (Soma); nelfinavir (Viracept); and others.

Magical use: Growing this plant around the outside of your home is said to prevent illness from entering.

Superstition and folklore: Feverfew has a long history of use in traditional and folk medicine, especially among Greek and early European herbalists.

Personal use: The plant is widely cultivated in large regions of the world and its importance as a medicinal plant is growing substantially with increasing and stronger reports in support of its multifarious therapeutic uses.

FIGWORT

Scientific Name(s): *Scrophularia nodosa*
Common Name(s): Carpenter's square; fiddlewood; fiddler; Crowdy Kit; brownwort; Bishops' Leaves; throatwort;

In the Middle Ages, the herb was thought to be one of the best medicinal plants to treat swellings and tumors. The herb was and is still used in salves and poultices to soothe inflamed skin in cases of psoriasis and eczema, and to heal burns; medieval herbalists used figwort to treat the 'king's evil', or scrofula – a tubercular disease of the lymph glands in the neck.

Simple: The bruised leaved were traditionally used as a poultice and applied to relieve burns and swelling.

CAUTION: DO NOT take figwort if you are taking diuretics or Lithium as figwort interacts unfavorably with these medications.

Magical uses: Figwort is a protective herb, said to ward off witches and to protect against the evil eye.

Superstition and folklore: During the thirteen months' siege of Rochelle by the army of Richelieu in 1628, the tuberous roots of this plant yielded support to the garrison for a considerable period, from which circumstance the French still call it *herbe du siège*. The taste and smell of the tubers are unpleasant, and they would never be resorted to for food except in times of famine.

Personal note: The herb was commonly known as carpenter's square because of its four-cornered stem.

FLAX

Scientific Name(s): *Linum usitatissimum*
Common Name(s): Linseed;

Fibres from the stems of flax, one of the world's oldest crop plants, were woven into linen by many ancient civilizations, including the Mesopotamians, Egyptians and Greeks. In Britain the plant has been cultivated since prehistoric times, and the fibres used to make ropes, nets, sacks, sails and even bow-strings. The 'fine linen' mentioned in the Bible has been satisfactorily proved to have been spun from flax; and it also furnished the garments of the Jewish High-Priests, as well as the curtains of the Tabernacle. Most religious houses in medieval England grew a patch of flax, from which they could make their own napkins and cloths. In the 8th-century Charlemagne demanded that his subjects ate flax seeds to maintain good health – although eating the seeds in quantity can be toxic! Inferior flax fibres, known as tow, were used as lamp wicks. Linseed oil, mixed with an equal quantity of lime water, known then as Carron Oil, was considered an excellent application for burns and scalds.

Simple: Today, flaxseed is available in the form of seeds, oils, powder, tablets, capsules, and flour. People use it as a dietary supplement to prevent constipation, diabetes, high cholesterol, heart disease, cancer, and several other conditions. [*Medical News Today*]

Magical use: In traditional Craft we use 'Fire, flax, fodder and frig' as a salutation/blessing, which refers to the hearth and home; to the clothes upon our backs; to the food on our plates and frig being slang for copulation. Reduced to 'FFF(F)' when used between Coveners.

Superstition and folklore: It was formerly believed that *flax* would only flower at the time of day on which it was originally sown. When dancing for *flax*, the higher the feet were raised from the floor, the higher would be the host's crop of flax next harvest.

Personal note: The ground meal was sometimes used fraudulently for adulterating pepper when this was an expensive commodity.

GARLIC

Scientific Name(s): *Allium sativum*

Common Name(s): Poor Man's Treacle; ransoms; wild wood garlic;

Garlic is native to Central Asia and northeastern Iran, and has long been a common seasoning worldwide, with a history of several thousand years of human consumption and use. It was known to the ancient Egyptians, and has been used both as a food flavoring and as a traditional medicine ever since. Garlic is mentioned in several Old English vocabularies of plants from the tenth to the fifteenth centuries, and is described by the herbalists of the sixteenth century from Turner (1548) onwards and is stated to have been grown in England before the year 1540.

Ransoms are also known as the 'wild wood garlic', but for its evil smell would rank among the most beautiful of our British plants. Its broad leaves are very similar to those of the lily-of-the-valley, and its star-like flowers are a dazzling white, *'but its odour is too strong to admit of it being picked for its beauty, and many woods, especially in the Cotswold Hills, are spots to be avoided when it is in flower, being so closely carpeted with the plants that every step taken brings out the offensive odour'* says Richard Mabey. Ramsons (*Allium ursinum*) grow in woods and has a very acrid taste and smell, but it also has very small bulbs, which would hardly render it of practical use – except for its popular use in witchcraft where it is offered as the cure for almost anything if you consult enough herbals! According to the Woodland Trust, ramsons are an ancient woodland indicator - meaning that this species can be used to aid identification of ancient woodland sites. In magic and ritual, wild garlic was thought to scare away venomous creatures and drive away moles!

Simple: In *Medical* News Today we find that people have used garlic as a food and medicine for more than 5000 years; for prevention of colds and 'flu, take one raw clove per day that has been bruised and chopped and infused in a cup of water and left to cool. Or obtain capsules from the local health shop.

CAUTION: Do not take garlic if you are on blood thinners as garlic is a potent blood thinner itself. **DO NOT** take garlic if you have been prescribed any of the following medications as garlic is known to interact with them and decrease their effectiveness: Isoniazid (Nydrazid, INH), AIDS medications including - nevirapine (Viramune), delavirdine (Rescriptor), and efavirenz (Sustiva), Saquinavir (Fortovase, Invirase), birth control pills, Cyclosporine (Neoral, Sandimmune), acetaminophen, chlorzoxazone (Parafon Forte), ethanol, theophylline, and drugs used for anesthesia during surgery such as enflurane (Ethrane), halothane (Fluothane), isoflurane (Forane), methoxyflurane (Penthrane), lovastatin (Mevacor), ketoconazole (Nizoral), itraconazole (Sporanox), fexofenadine (Allegra), and triazolam (Halcion).

Magical use: Peeled garlic cloves can be placed in doorways and around the house for protection from illness and to keep evil at bay - especially in new homes. Use an infusion in spray form around the outside of the house for protection.

Superstition and folklore: In folklore, garlic has been regarded as a force for both good and evil. In Europe, many cultures have used garlic for protection, perhaps owing to its reputation in folk medicine. Central European folk beliefs considered garlic a powerful ward against demons, werewolves, and vampires. To ward off vampires, garlic could be worn about the neck, hung in windows, or rubbed on chimneys, locks and keyholes. Garlic was also the principal ingredient in the famous 'Four thieves vinegar' that was reputed to keep the plague at bay.

Personal note: In Cole's *Art of Simpling* we are told that cocks which have been fed on garlic are 'most stout to fight' ...

GOOSEBERRY

Scientific Name(s): *Ribes uva-crispa*
Common Name(s): Goosegogs;

Culpeper wrote that the fruit was '*cooling and astringent, creating an appetite, and quenching thirst*'; while a decoction of the leaves cool hot swellings and inflammations' and applied externally as a dressing, to heal wounds. And what better for a perfect summer pudding than a Gooseberry Fool - smooth, timeless and soothing, the fool is simply crushed fruits folded into whipped cream.

Simple: Gooseberries are low in calories and fat, yet packed with nutrients including Vitamin C (a powerful antioxidant and vital to our nervous system, immune system, and skin); Vitamin B5 (necessary for creating fatty acids), while vitamin B6, which many enzymes and cells in our bodies need to function, helps convert food into energy. Copper is important for our heart, blood vessels, immune system, and brain; meanwhile, manganese supports metabolism, bone formation, reproduction, and immune response, whereas potassium is essential for normal cell function. [*Heathline*]

Magical use: Gooseberries have sympathetic magical qualities, representing that which is of tasteful and the divine influence, and for our greater good.

Superstition and folklore: According to an old custom, pricking a stye or wart with a gooseberry thorn will cause it to disappear!

Personal note: Although a native to Britain, the gooseberry was rarely grown in medieval English gardens.

GORSE

Scientific Name(s): *Ulex europaeus*
Common Name(s): Furze; whin; prickly broom; ruffet; frey; goss;

A native to Britain, its name is derived from the Old English for a 'waste place', probably because it flourishes on the light soil of wild and exposed heathland. It was used for fuel, as a hedging to protect livestock from predators, and for hanging washing over (the dense thorns stopped it from blowing away). The golden-yellow flowers have a powerful scent, perfuming the air. They open from early spring up to autumn, but bushes are to be found in blossom practically the whole year round.

Simple: Gorse had surprisingly few medicinal uses, though its flowers have been used in the past as a treatment of jaundice, scarlet fever, diarrhoea and kidney stones. Mixed with lard, the flowers are used to make Whitby gorse salve to treat chapped and roughened hands of the fishermen. Method: Melt a lump of lard gently and add as many gorse flowers as the lard will take. Leave overnight in a warm place for the lard to absorb the goodness from the flowers. Ideally, the mixture should be just warm enough to keep the lard liquid. Next day re-melt the mixture, strain out the flowers through muslin, then add more fresh flowers and leave overnight again. Repeat this several times until the lard has taken on a good yellow colour from the flowers; then it is ready to use. [*The Secret People*]

Magical use: Protection against evil; restoration of faith, hope and optimism; gathering of strength. It also attracts gold, so it is used in money spells. Protects against negativity and dark magic. Carve the name 'Gorse' into a gold or yellow candle. Face east, light the candle, and meditate on the light. Ask for protection, money, love, or whatever it has to offer that you desire.

Superstition and folklore: Gorse was considered unlucky, and if allowed into the house, death or similar misfortune would follow. It had an old reputation as an insecticide: *Against fleas, take this same wort, with its seed, sodden; sprinkle it into the house; it killeth the fleas.*

Personal note: A bit of any unruly character but it flowers all year round, which gave rise to the popular sayings: *When gorse is out of bloom, kissing's out of season.* I have several large bushes in the hedge where, left to their own devices, they seed themselves and produces a wonderful springtime display. When the weather warms up and the bees are active it is worth going out to watch them working the gorse because the flower is specially designed to make best use of them for pollination.

GROUNDSEL

Scientific Name(s): *Senecio vulgaris*
Common Name(s): Ground glutton; Old-man-in-the-spring; simson; sention;

Although a common weed, groundsel has been valued as a healing herb since at least Roman times. In the Middle Ages it was used as a poultice for inflammation, haemorrhoids and gout. As a plant that is reported to be both poisonous for human ingestion and also medicinal, it does not seem to be recommended very often since 1931, when it was recommended as a diaphoretic, an antiscorbutic, a purgative, a diuretic and an anthelmintic; which was a demotion as it was previously suggested for the expelling of kidney stones by Pedanius Dioscorides in the 1st century; for use as poultices by John Gerard in the late 16th-century and as a cure for epilepsy by Nicholas Culpeper in the 17th-century.

Groundsel, so well-known as a troublesome weed, is connected in the minds of most of us with caged birds, and probably few people are aware that it has any other use except as a favourite food for the canary. And yet in former days, groundsel *was* a popular herbal remedy, is still employed in some country districts, and forms an item in the stock of the modern herbalist, though it is not given a place in the British Pharmacopoeia. It was formerly much used for poultices and reckoned good for sickness of the stomach. A weak infusion of the plant is now sometimes given as a simple and easy purgative, and a strong infusion as an emetic.

Simple: Groundsel in an old-fashioned remedy for chapped hands. If boiling water be poured on the fresh plant, the liquid forms a pleasant swab for the skin and will remove roughness. [*Mrs. Grieve's Modern Herbal*]

CAUTION: Groundsel may increase the toxic effect of the following medications, and should not be taken with them: carbamazepine (Tegretol), phenobarbital, phenytoin (Dilantin), rifampin, and rifabutin (Mycobutin).

Magical use: In the hands of herbal simplers groundsel formerly held high rank as a herb of power. According to Scott Cunningham's *Encyclopaedia of Magical Herbs* it was carried as an amulet against toothache.

Superstition and folklore: Groundsel has a place in Irish folk lore as: *A little plant called groundsel was a good cure for a headache.*

Another old herbalist tells us that the fresh roots smelled when first taken out of the ground are an immediate cure for many forms of headache. But the root must not be dug up with a tool that has any iron in its composition.

Personal note: Some of the old authorities claimed that groundsel was especially good for such wounds as had been caused by being struck by iron.

GUELDER ROSE

Scientific Name(s): *Viburnum opulus*
Common Name(s): Dogberry; crampbark; snowball tree; Whitsun rose; rose elder;

An attractive native shrub often seen in country hedgerows. It has maple-like leaves and beautiful fragrant white lace-cap flowers in the spring, followed by clusters of translucent red berries in early autumn. It is a great addition to a wildlife fruiting hedgerow. In herbal practice in this country, its administration in decoction and infusion, as well as the fluid extract and compound tincture has long been recommended. It has been employed with benefit in all nervous complaints and debility and used with success in cramps and spasms of all kinds, in convulsions, fits and lockjaw, and also in palpitation, heart disease and rheumatism. The ancient Celts had seven herbs that were valued as sacred: dandelion, comfrey, mugwort, burdock, mistletoe, nettle, and the guelder rose.

The cycle of the guelder rose begins with the *white* flowers of the Maiden, Olwen of the White Track, although her more usual flower is the May (hawthorn or whitethorn). Just after Lammas the fruits ripen into the bright *red* berries of the Mother. The dried fruits – if the birds haven't had them – turn to the *black* of the Wise One, the Crone who holds the wisdom of the Ancestors. Over the winter, the guelder rose stand leafless, its branches dark against the winter sun, sparkling with bright red berries until midwinter when all turn black in preparation for rebirth.

Simple: Guelder rose is traditionally used to treat cramp, hence the plant's common names 'crampbark' or 'crampbush' It is also used as a sedative remedy for nervous conditions. Bathe in a strong decoction of the flowers for various skin conditions.

Magical use: Use in spells/charms for rebirth, reawakening, reincarnation, regeneration, renewal, revival. return, reappearance, reoccurrence, resume, revisit, restore, return, repay, pay back, reimburse, refund, give back, change, new beginning, new start, coming again, homecoming and arrival.

Superstition and folklore: Guelder rose is one of the national symbols of Ukraine and is mentioned in many folk songs and featured in art and embroidery.

Personal note: Guelder rose is an ancient-woodland indicator. If we spot it while we're out exploring, it could be a sign we're standing in a rare and special habitat.

HAREBELL

Scientific Name(s): *Campanula rotundifolia*
Common Name(s): Scottish bluebell; Old man's bells; Dead men's bells;

Harebell roots were applied by medieval physicians as a compress to heal wounds, staunch bleeding and reduce inflammations. The root has been chewed in the treatment of heart and lung problems; an infusion of the roots has been used as ear drops for a sore ear; a decoction of the plant has been drunk or used as a wash in the treatment of sore eyes. There are also numerous references to harebells actually ringing, and this old belief is mentioned in many places, for example in a song from 1911, *An Autumn Song* with lyrics by Fred G Bowles:

How soon the Autumn day is done,
The briefer light, the lower sun
Pale hare-bells ringing in the wood,

A somewhat evocative image and possibly a faint echo of an older, more sinister belief about harebells ringing because another of their country names was dead men's bells referring to the idea that to hear them ringing was an extremely ill omen. And, once again when we follow the references to harebells ringing, it is not long before we find the Faere Folk – not the cute versions of modern pop culture but those clearly linked to the older and darker associations the flower has with supernatural beings.

Simple: None.

Magical use: The flower was associated with witches (who were said to transform themselves into hares by using the juice from the plant); the Faere Folk and other supernatural beings.

Superstition and folklore: It was said that the harebell was best avoided as it was believed to belong to the Devil, hence its common name Old man's bells.

Personal note: The harebell is the emblem of the MacDonald's, and its flower was said to provide a blue dye that was used to colour the wool for tartans

HAWTHORN

Scientific Name(s): *Cratageus oxyacantha*
Common Name(s): May; whitethorn; hagthorn; bread and cheese;

In European traditions, the hawthorn is immersed with mystery and folklore. In the spring its branches are filled with white to pink blossoms that attract countless pollinators. The scent of the flowers has been described as everything from death and decay to divine and erotic. Depending on the location, hawthorn is often found blooming in late April and early May and has long been associated with *Beltaine,* the cross-quarter holiday between the Spring Equinox and Summer Solstice. Medicinally it can be classified with a handful of medicinal herbal actions, such as anti-hypertensive, anti-anginal, or anti-cholesterolemic and as a herb that nourishes and protects the heart. Long-term and short-term studies have shown that the hawthorn offers many benefits for people who already have mild to moderate heart disease.

Simple: The flowering tops of fresh hawthorn are used in a daily infusion for relieving heart problems. Use 1 teaspoon of the dried herb, or 1½ teaspoons of the fresh herb, to 1 cup of boiling water steeped for 10 minutes.

DANGER: DO NOT take hawthorn if you have been prescribed Digoxin (Lanoxin), beta-blockers, Calcium channel blockers, Phosphodiesterase-5 Inhibitors, or Nitrates (Nitroglycerine, (Nitro-Bid, Nitro-Dur, Nitrostat) and isosorbide (Imdur, Isordil, Sorbitrate)). Hawthorn mixed with these medications is dangerous and may cause life-threatening complications.

Magical use: Placed around doors and windows, hawthorn will prevent people from entering our home in an astral state. It will also prevent spirits from entering a place. Adding hawthorn to an amulet will protect the bearer from malign spirits and harmful magic.

Superstition and folklore: Although the ancient Greeks and Romans brought cuttings into the home to ward off evil spirits, in Britain it was the height of bad luck to bring the blossom into the house.

Personal note: Regardless of what it says on the calendar, *if the hawthorn's not in bloom, it ain't Beltaine!*

HEATHER

Scientific Name(s): *Calluna vulgaris*
Common Name(s): Ling;

A native to Britain, heather grows extensively on acid moorland and heathland; its botanical name *Calluna* derives from the Greek of 'to brush', a reminder that bundles of heather twigs were used to make brushes and brooms. 'Ling' is derived from the Old English for fire, and refers to the plant's importance as a fuel in Anglo-Saxon times. The plant is also highly medicinal, and for generations many cultures have been chopping up the leaves and petals of the flower and preparing potent teas.

purple heather
smudges eventide fire
solstice sun wanes

Simple: Heather tea benefits a variety of functions in the body, and is an excellent way of cleansing toxins from organs and relieving inflammatory pains. Heather tops make a pleasant tea, which is mildly sedative and said to help depression, insomnia and nervous exhaustion. Use 2-3 teaspoons of fresh flowers to a cup of boiling water and infuse for about five minutes.

Magical use: Heather can be used in spells relating to new beginnings, and self-discovery, enhancing physical beauty and bringing a peaceful resolution to any conflict. It is also used at initiations. Keeping heather about the house and growing in the garden will attract friendly spirits and will bring peace to the household. Carrying heather will attract positive energies, general good luck and protect against rape and other violent assaults, making it useful for traveling sachets.

Superstition and folklore: In Scotland, farmers carried torches of burning heather around their fields before midsummer to ensure good crops and around their cattle to ensure their fertility.

Personal note: As the flowers are a rich source of nectar for honey, beekeepers often placed their hives amidst the heather moorland.

HERB BENNET

Scientific Name(s): *Geum urbanum*
Common Name(s): Wood Avens; colewort; St. Benedict's Herb;

A perennial plant in the rose family (*Rosaceae*), which grows in shady places such as woodland edges and near hedgerows; the hermaphrodite flowers are scented and pollinated by bees. The fruits have burrs, which are used for dispersal by getting caught in the fur of rabbits and other animals. In the 16th-century, wood avens was a common kitchen herb in Central Europe and was often grown in herb gardens. The fresh leaves give a slight but pleasant flavour to salads, soups, and stews, while the ground rhizome can be used as a substitute for cloves as a spice for soups and broths. This is an astringent *herb*, used principally to treat problems affecting the mouth, throat and gastro-intestinal tract; it tightens up soft gums and heals mouth ulcers.

Simple: The plant's astringent effect also explains its traditional uses as a gargle or mouthwash to treat a sore throat and bad breath. Add ½-1 teaspoon of the crushed root in a cup of cold water, then boil and simmer for 5 minutes.

Magical use: The herb was often worn as a protective amulet or stored in homes and other buildings to keep them safe.

Superstition and folklore: In folklore, wood avens was credited with the power to keep the devil at bay and protect against evil spirits. It was also believed that the herb could offer protection against rabid dogs and snakebites.

Personal note: In the 1100s Hildegard of Bingen, the German Benedictine abbess, writer, composer and philosopher, nicknamed the plant *benedicta*, which means 'the blessed'.

HERB ROBERT

Scientific Name(s): *Geranium robertianum*
Common Name(s): Red robin; Death come quickly; storksbill; fox

geranium; Stinking Bob; Squinter-pip (Shropshire); crow's foot;

Herb Robert has been used in the folk medicine of several countries, often as a treatment for diarrhoea; to improve functioning of the liver and gallbladder; for toothache and nosebleeds; and as a vulnerary (useful in healing wounds). The name has been explained as a reference to abbot and herbalist Fr. Robert, a French Abbot of Molerne, who had legendary medical skills, probably thanks to this plant. Freshly picked leaves have an odor resembling burning tires when crushed, and if they are rubbed on the body the smell is said to repel mosquitoes! Herb Robert's strong distinctive smell acts as an insect deterrent making it a good companion plant in the garden for vegetables and flowers. Plants seem to grow well next to it. The plant is used for diarrhoea, to improve functioning of the liver and gallbladder, to reduce swelling (inflammation) of the kidney, bladder, and gallbladder, and to prevent the formation of stones in the kidney, bladder. Some people use it as a mouthwash or gargle.

Simple: For an infusion do not **use tap water**. Use mineral water, or, better, spring water that must not be older than 48 hours. In a cup of water put one tablespoon of uncrushed dried leaves and flowers, to soak overnight; filtered in the morning and scald the remaining plant with another cup of water before using as a mouthwash.

Magical use: Used in herbal magic and green *witchcraft* for self-realization, confidence, courage and love.

Superstition and folklore: The association with death was enhanced by the name Robert, a folk name for a devilish sprite who liked to cause trouble for people.

Personal note: A pretty plant that not out of place in any garden with its bright pink flowers, red stems and fern-like leaves.

HONEY

Being essentially of floral origin, and as a vegetable product endowed with curative properties, honey may be fairly ranked among herbal Simples. Indeed, it is the nectar of flowers, partaking attributes, according to the species of plant from which it is produced, wrote W T Fernie in Herbal Simples.

The *health benefits* of *honey* include *healing* wounds and fighting off infections and raw honey has been used as a folk remedy throughout history - having a variety of health benefits and medical uses. Its use in hospitals as a treatment for wounds dates back to the ancient Egyptians, Assyrians, Chinese, Greeks and Romans who all employed honey for wounds; as did the *Russians* in *World War I* to prevent *wound infection* and to accelerate healing. Many of the health benefits are specific to raw, or unpasteurized honey - and as most of the honey we find in grocery stores is pasteurized, stock up with locally produced honey from the health shop or farmer's market.

Simple: A hot honey and lemon drink is the perfect treatment for a sore throat and a cold. Place the juice of a lemon with a teaspoon of honey in a cup of hot water. It will protect against allergies if we eat just a teaspoon of locally sourced honey each day - and it also has a number of magical properties.

DANGER: DO NOT give to infants under the age of twelve months as it may cause infant botulism, a potentially deadly form of food poisoning.

Magical use: Some ancient cultures used honey in embalming procedures and it was often thought appropriate to leave offerings of honey at a gravesite. Include it in spell-work for bringing and keeping two things together.

Superstition and folklore: The folklore of a number of societies indicates that a blend of honey and milk is an acceptable offering to a deity.

Personal note: Most forms of *honey* have antibacterial *properties.*

HONEYSUCKLE

Scientific Name(s): *Lonicera periclymenum*
Common Name(s): *Woodbine;*

Although honeysuckle grew wild all over Britain, it was cultivated in gardens for its rich fragrance and Culpeper said of it:

> *Honeysuckles are cleansing, consuming and digesting, and therefore no way fit for inflammations. Take a leaf and chew it in your mouth and you will quickly find it likelier to cause a sore mouth and throat than cure it. If it be not good for this, what is it good for? It is good for something, for God and nature made nothing in vain. It is a herb of Mercury, and appropriated to the lungs; the celestial Crab claims dominion over it, neither is it a foe to the Lion; if the lungs be afflicted by Jupiter, this is your cure. It is fitting a conserve made of the flowers should be kept in every gentlewoman's house; I know no better cure for the asthma than this besides it takes away the evil of the spleen: provokes urine, procures speedy delivery of women in travail, relieves cramps, convulsions, and palsies, and whatsoever griefs come of cold or obstructed perspiration; if you make use of it as an ointment, it will clear the skin of morphew, freckles, and sunburnings, or whatever else discolours it, and then the maids will love it. Authors say, the flowers are of more effect than the leaves, and that is true: but they say the seeds are the least effectual of all. But there is a vital spirit in every seed to beget its like; there is a greater heat in the seed than any other part of the plant; and heat is the mother of action.*

Honeysuckle has long been used in teas, tinctures, flower water and ointments but the only remedy with instructions for use is an old one from John Evelyn (1792), who mentions using the spring buds of honeysuckle '*in the same manner and purposes as elderflower'*. The sturdy stems of honeysuckle have been used to make rope as far back as the Bronze Age, and in parts of Britain are still commonly made into bridles and harnesses for pack ponies. The name honeysuckle comes from the tradition of children biting off the ends of the flowers to enjoy the drops of nectar inside.

Simple: Honeysuckle tea has a lovely pale celadon colour, a light floral scent, and a surprisingly sweet flavor made from gently crushed flowers in a jug or cup and topped up with hot water. Put the pitcher in the refrigerator overnight, or at least 6-8 hours; strain the flowers out and enjoy your honeysuckle tea over ice. Take to sooth digestive disorders and upper respiratory tract infections. Don't add honey before tasting as it's incredibly sweet all by itself; add a squeeze of lemon if you don't like sweet tea.

DANGER: DO NOT take if you have been prescribed anticoagulant or antiplatelet medications. Honeysuckle interacts with anticoagulant and antiplatelet drugs and may cause you to disproportionately bruise or haemorrhage.

Magical use: Honeysuckle flowers may be used in spells designed to determine the true worth of a person or thing. They may be burned in a censer or steep the flowers in wine, strain, and drink. The scent of honeysuckle is said to clear the mind, stimulate psychic powers, sharpen intuition, encourage psychic dreams, sweeten any mood and stimulate generosity. A flower rubbed on the forehead is believed to increase psychic abilities.

Superstition and folklore: Tradition says that if the flowers are placed in a girl's bedroom, she will dream of love; and if brought into the house, there will soon be a wedding.

Personal note: Honeysuckle is not intended for long-term use. While the flowers are low in toxicity, the fruits, leaves, and stems are more dangerous. Symptoms of poisoning include extreme tiredness, drowsiness, dilated pupils, and photosensitivity.

HOREHOUND

Scientific Name(s): *Marrubium vulgate*
Common Name(s): White horehound;

The plant has long been cultivated to treat various ailments, especially coughs, catarrh, asthma and respiratory complaints; it was especially valued by the Greeks and the Romans, as well as the ancient Egyptians. A native to Britain, it was known to the Anglo-Saxons – and is said to be one of the bitter Passover herbs since the botanical name is derived from the Hebrew for 'bitter juice'. Its leaves were used to clean milk pails and, soaked in fresh milk, to kill flies. The leaves and flowering tops were used as flavouring for beverages and candies, and infusions or extracts of horehound in the form of syrups, teas, or lozenges were sometimes used in herbal remedies for coughs and minor pulmonary disturbances.

Simple: Place a teaspoon of horehound leaves per cup inside your teapot. Pour the boiling water over the leaves. And then allow to steep for about 5 minutes. The longer you let it steep, the stronger your tea will become.

Magical use: When utilized magically, it is said to keep off wild animals and packs of dogs. Folks who use it for protection sprinkle the dried leaves around the perimeter of their property; it may be made into an infusion spray to protect the home, in addition to sprinkling the dried leaves onto the floor and sweeping them out the door.

Superstition and folklore: According to John Gower in Book 7 of the *Confessio Amantis (c.1386)*, this plant was the herb of the fourth star of Nectanebus' astrology, Capella. Gower used the older name, Alhaiot (VII:1338).

Personal note: Horehound is an invasive plant much like the mints. It's a good idea to plant it in an area with plenty of room or to confine it in a pot. Cut off the flowers to minimize the spread of the plant as horehound seeds itself. The home gardener needs only two or three plants for personal use.

HORSETAIL

Scientific Name(s): *Equiselum arvense*
Common Name (s): Shave-grass. bottle-brush. Paddock-pipes. Dutch Rushes; pewterwort;

Large plants of this order probably formed a great proportion of the vegetation during the Carboniferous period, the well-known fossils calamites being the stems of gigantic *Equisetaceae*, which in this period attained their maximum development - those now existing being mere dwarfish representatives. According to Mrs. Grieve:

> *The barren stems only are used medicinally, appearing after the fruiting stems have died down, and are used in their entirety, cut off just above the root. The herb is used either fresh or dried, but is said to be most efficacious when fresh.*

Simple: An externally application will stop the bleeding of wounds and quickly heal them. To prepare a decoction for use in making a cataplasm (poultice) or compress, boil 2½ teaspoons herb in 1 pint water for 10-15 minutes. Cataplasm: Semi-solid paste prepared from horsetail aqueous decoction for a moist-heat direct application to the skin; used like a poultice to remove deep-seated inflammation. Saturate a stupe (a piece of soft cloth or cotton wool dipped in hot water); fold and apply firmly to relieve pain or inflammation. [*A Modern Herbal*]
DANGER: DO NOT take horsetail if you have been prescribed lithium as it may slow down the absorption of lithium by the liver, resulting in dangerous levels being stored in the body and severe side effects.
Magical use: Horsetail strengthens resolve and defines

boundaries. It can be used to make affirmations and commitments and to protect one's psychic space against unwanted intrusions. It helps to cleanse unwanted emotional rubble and debris from the system. It is an herb of Saturn and Time since it has been around long before man walked the earth.

Superstition and folklore: Horsetail's reedy exterior and silica content have made it a popular metal polisher and natural abrasive cleanser. One species is so rich in silica that it was imported from Holland for the purpose of polishing metal, hence the nickname Dutch rushes. Another nickname is pewterwort, so named because it was used to scour pewter. Dairy maids of England used horsetail to scour their milk pails, while early Americans used it to scrub their metal pots and pans.

Personal note: This plant is a 'living fossil', the only living genus of the entire subclass *Equisetidae*, which for over 100 million years was much more diverse and dominated the understory of late Paleozoic forests. Some were large trees reaching to 98 feet tall.

HOUND'S TONGUE

Scientific Name(s): *Cynoglossum officinale*
Common Name(s): Gypsy flower; rats-and-mice;

A native of Britain, hound's tongue grew wild in grassland and on the edge of woodland throughout much of the country. The plant was widely valued for its soothing, healing and pain-killing properties in the treatment of cuts, bruised, burns, sores and diseases. Culpeper recommended it for coughs and colds, as well as to cure the bite of mad dogs, baldness and venereal disease! Hound's tongue is mildly poisonous and should be handled with care since the plant also has narcotic tendencies.

Simple: Steep one teaspoon of the dried root or herb in a cup of water and transfer to a small glass spray bottle. Keep refrigerated and use the spray around areas where vermin are evident.

Magical use: According to the *Herbalist Almanac*, if hound's tongue is gathered when the sap is full of vigour, bruise it with a hammer and lay it about the house, barn or granary that is infested with rats or mice – and they will 'shift their quarters'.

Superstition and folklore: Ancient superstition held that dogs would be silenced and unable to bark at any person who placed a piece of the herb under their big toe.

Personal note: Because of its pungent smell, it was commonly known as 'rats-and-mice' because the bruised leaves have a disagreeable 'mousy' or musty odour.

HOUSELEEK

Scientific Name(s): *Sempervivum tectorum*
Common Name(s): Sengren; liveforever; Hen and chicks;

A common garden plant that the Anglo-Saxons knew as *leac* or leek. It has been used historically and is used presently for purported health benefits. Common herbal uses are stopping bad cases of diarrhoea by drinking the juice of the leaf or eating the leaves directly, and the juice is commonly applied directly to the skin for many of the same uses as aloe vera - such as burns, warts and insect bites. It is furthermore said to bring relief in cases of swellings and water retention. The famous English herbalist Culpeper wrote:

> *Our ordinary Houseleek is good for all inward heats, as well as outward, and in the eyes or other parts of the body: a posset made of the juice is singularly good in all hot agues, for it cooleth and tempereth the blood and spirits and quencheth the thirst; and is also good to stay all deflection or sharp and salt rheums in the eyes, the juice being dropped into them. If the juice be dropped into the ears, it easeth pain.... It cooleth and restraineth all hot inflammations St. Anthony's fire, scaldings and burnings, the shingles, fretting*

ulcers, ringworms and the like; and much easeth the pain and the gout.

Simple: Fresh bruised leaves can be used for a cooling application on the forehead to treat feverish symptoms and headaches; can also be applied to burns, insect bites and other skin problems, An infusion of the leaves can be made with 1 teaspoon of leaves to one cup of water.

Magical use: Charlemagne ordered that the plant be grown throughout his empire for its magical properties, which included keeping witches and evil spirits away.

Superstition and folklore: It was traditionally believed that lightning would never strike a building with houseleeks growing on the roof.

Personal note: The young evergreen leaves were added to medieval salads, or eaten as a vegetable.

HYSSOP

Scientific Name(s): *Hyssopus officinalis*
Common Name(s): Hyssop;

Hippocrates recommended hyssop for chest complaints, while the *Ussopos* of Dioscorides, was named from the holy herb *azob*, used for cleansing sacred places – now thought to be marjoram, The green herb, bruised and applied as a dressing, is found to heal bruises and cuts promptly. As a kitchen herb it has gone out of use because of its strong flavor - but on account of its aroma it was formerly employed as a strewing herb.

Simple: A hyssop infusion is relaxing and makes a very pleasant tea for nervous exhaustion. Infuse 1 teaspoon dried hyssop leaves and flowers in 1 covered cup of boiling water for 10 minutes, Strain and sweeten with honey. Drink up to 2 cups per day.

Magical use: Its botanical name is derived from the Greek for a holy herb, referring to its ancient use in purifying ceremonies, and in the cleansing of sacred areas.

Superstition and folklore: Hyssop was also strewn on the floor in churches and infirmaries since it was reputed to prevent the spread of infectious diseases.

Personal note: It was another of the bitter herbs traditionally eaten by the Jews at the Passover.

IRIS: YELLOW FLAG

Scientific Name(s): *Iris pseudacorus*
Common Name(s): Orris root; Fleur-de-lys;

The violet-scented, powered root of orris has been used in perfumery and cosmetics since ancient Egyptian times; it was also put in wardrobes to sweeten linen. Orris is harvested in Italy and has been a traditional fixative for scent since ancient Greece. Lyte says *'the Iris is knowen of the clothworkers and drapers, for with these rootes they use to trimme their clothes to make them sweete and pleasant'*. This was probably the 'swete clothe' so celebrated in the reign of Elizabeth. [*A Modern Herbal*]

Simple: None

Magical use: As a Moon plant, orris root is good for digging deep into the Moon-ruled subconscious and uprooting what is hidden; like any Moon herb, it can also be used in divination and dreamwork. Orris root is popular in love charms and used in sachets, powders or amulets designed to attract the opposite sex. In Japan, it was used to ward off evil spirits.

Superstition and folklore: Pliny wrote that those who intend to dig up the root must first offer

a libation to please the earth. They then draw three circles around it with the point of a sword, pull it up and raise it to the heavens. It is hot by nature, and when handled raises burn-like blisters. It is essential that those who gather it should be chaste.

Personal note: The fleur-de-lys was adopted as an emblem by Louis VII of France in the second crusade against the Saracens.

IVY

Scientific Name(s): *Hedera helix*
Common Name(s): English ivy;

Found in woods and along walls, upon trees and climbing stone walls of houses, churches, etc., English ivy is an evergreen vine that grows to the length of over 50 feet; it bears air roots along its length that enables it to cling to smooth surfaces. The small green, or yellowish-green flowers appear in umbels from August to October and the fruit is a black berry, ripening in winter to provide essential food source for wild life. Ivy was in high esteem among the ancients. Its leaves formed the poet's crown, as well as the wreath of Bacchus, to whom the plant was dedicated, probably because of the practice of binding the brow with ivy leaves to prevent intoxication, a quality formerly attributed to the plant. We are told by old writers that the effects of intoxication by wine are removed if a handful of ivy leaves are bruised and gently boiled in wine and drunk. The Greek priests presented a wreath of ivy to newly-married persons, and the ivy has throughout the ages been regarded as the emblem of fidelity. The custom of decorating houses and churches with the leaves at Christmas was forbidden by one of the early Councils of the Church, on account of its pagan associations, but the custom still remains.

Simple: English ivy is used primarily for external use only as a wash for sores, burns, cuts, dandruff and other skin problems. Use one teaspoon of leaves to one cup of cold water; let it stand for eight hours and only use externally.

Magical use: Although ivy was believed to be a protective magical plant, in some areas of England it was considered unlucky to bring it into the house.

Superstition and folklore: During the Middle Ages the plant was reputed to be the enemy of the vine and that drinking from ivy-wood cups would prevent drunkenness.

Personal note: All parts of the ivy are poisonous although a poultice of the leaves was used to treat burns, scalds, sores, wounds and painful swellings in medieval times.

LADY'S MANTLE

Scientific Name(s): *Alchemilla vulgaris*
Common Name(s): Lion's foot; bear's foot; Nine Hooks; stellaria; (French) *Pied-de-lion;*

The common Lady's Mantle is generally distributed over Britain, but more especially in the colder districts and on high-lying ground, being found up to an altitude of 3,600 feet in the Scottish Highlands. It is indeed essentially a plant of the north, freely found beyond the Arctic circle in Europe, Asia and also in Greenland and Labrador, and only on high mountain ranges, such as the Himalaya, if found in southern latitudes. Herbalists prescribe it for a variety of conditions. 'Lady's mantle' is a good description, for it is chiefly a herb for women; it is anti-inflammatory and astringent, and has properties that are good for regulating menstruation. While Culpeper says of it:

> *Lady's Mantle is very proper for inflamed wounds and to stay bleeding, vomitings, fluxes of all sorts, bruises by falls and ruptures. It is one of the most singular wound herbs and therefore highly prized and praised, used in all wounds inward and outward, to drink a decoction thereof and wash the wounds therewith, or dip tents* therein and put them into the wounds which wonderfully drieth up all humidity of the sores and abateth all inflammations*

cureth old sores, though fistulous and hollow.

*A conical, expansible plug of soft material for dilating an orifice or for keeping a wound open, so as to prevent its healing except at the bottom.

Simple: The plant can be used for gynaecological disorders; or herbal tea mixtures for the winter, when the astringent properties are good for sore throats. Taken internally as an infusion, use 1 oz of the dried herb or 1½ oz of the fresh herb to 1 pint of boiling water in teacupful doses as required. Poultices can be made of the young leaves for minor cuts. Mashed leaves under a plaster will do wonders overnight for those garden injuries that can leave hands looking battered.

Magical use: The generic name *Alchemilla* is derived from the Arabic word *Alkemelych* (alchemy), and was bestowed on it, according to some old writers, because of the wonder-working powers of the plant. Others held that the alchemical virtues lay in the subtle influence the foliage imparted to the dewdrops that lay in its furrowed leaves and in the little cup formed by its joined stipules, these dewdrops constituting part of many mystic potions. It was thought that the water droplets that formed on the leaves were the purest form of water and might turn base metals into gold. It was considered a magical plant – and still is.

Superstition and folklore: The plant was believed to have the power to restore female beauty, no matter how faded.

Personal note: The plant is of graceful growth and though only a foot high and green throughout- flowers, stem and leaves alike, and therefore inconspicuous - the rich form of its foliage and the beautiful shape of its clustering blossoms make it worthy of notice. [*A Modern Herbal*]

LAVENDER

Scientific Name(s): *Lavendula officinalis* or *Lavandula augustifolia*
Common Name(s): Old English lavender;

In Spain and Portugal, lavender was traditionally strewn on the floor of churches or thrown into bonfires to avert evil spirits on St. John's Day; in Tuscany, pinning a sprig of lavender to your shirt is a traditional ward against the evil eye. All the forms of lavender are much visited by bees and prove a good source of honey but the all-round favourites are Old English and French varieties. Lavender deters fleas and moths. Place sachets of lavender buds or lavender wands in cupboards and closets or stuff them into pet bedding to help deter pests from these areas. Also, put sachets of lavender in your dryer to scent your laundry. These can be reused several times.

Simple: Lavender is useful for headaches and insomnia by using a room-spray made by simply infusing lavender flowers in water. An infusion of lavender tops, made in moderate strength, is excellent to relieve headache from fatigue and exhaustion, giving the same relief as the application of lavender water to the temples. Measure 2 tablespoons lavender buds for each cup boiling water and steep for 30 minutes. Strain liquid into a small glass spray bottle and keep in the refrigerator.

CAUTION: DO NOT take lavender if you have been prescribed barbiturates, chloral hydrate, or any of the following medications: clonazepam (Klonopin), lorazepam (Ativan), phenobarbital (Donnatal), and zolpidem (Ambien) as their effectiveness will be increased causing excessive sleepiness.

Magical use: The world of plants has long been inspiring and magical to many cultures. Plant lavender around your house to keep away bad luck/evil spirits and, always plant lavender at your front gate for good fortune.

Superstition and folklore: Couples who place lavender flowers between their bed sheets will never quarrel.

Personal note: The 'straw', completely freed from the flowers, if burnt for incense the stalks diffuse a powerful, but agreeable odour.

LEMON

Scientific Name(s): *Citrus limon*
Common Name(s): Limon;

The lemon is probably the most valuable of all fruit for preserving health. English ships were required by law to carry sufficient lemon or lime juice for every seaman to have an ounce daily after being ten days at sea to prevent scurvy. As a rich source of vitamin C, lemon juice protects the body from immune system deficiencies. Drinking lemon juice with warm water every morning helps in maintaining the pH balance of the body. With its powerful antibacterial properties, lemon juice helps fight infections and acts as a detoxifying agent. Lemon juice is also an effective way to reduce weight as it increases the body's metabolic rate.

Simple: The juice (or two slices) added to a cup of hot water is an excellent gargle for sore throats; honey and lemon infusions are disinfecting and mildly expectorant for colds and fevers.

Magical use: Lemon juice mixed with water is used for magically cleansing ritual objects that have been brought in from outside; this wash ensures that all negativity has been removed from the object in question.

Superstition and folklore: By keeping a whole lemon in a glass of water we come to know about the negative or positive vibes in our homes or workplace wherever it's kept. If the lemon floats, be assured that there is positive around and in case the lemon sinks to the bottom then it's a bit disconcerting as there is negativity around.

Personal note: These Mediterranean plants have very fragrant blossom and attractive fruits all year round. A wonderful plant for a cool conservatory in winter and outdoors on the patio in summer. Fragrant leaves, flowers and edible fruit!

LEMON BALM

Scientific Name(s): *Melissa officinalis*
Common Name(s): Melissa; sweet balm; balm mint; bee balm; blue balm; cure-all; dropsy plant; garden balm;

Lemon balm has a long history, dating back to ancient Turkey where it was planted near bee hives to encourage the bees to return home to the hive rather than swarm away. It has been used 'to make the heart merry' since ancient times and modern clinical trials have clearly demonstrated lemon balm's ability to calm nervous tension. An excellent herb for restlessness, agitation and irritability especially associated with headaches or gastric upset. Take after a meal to aid digestion and before bed to prevent insomnia and nightmares.

Simple: Infuse 2 fresh leaves in a cup of boiling water. Cover and steep for 10 minutes.
CAUTION: DO NOT take if you are prescribed sedatives including clonazepam (Klonopin), lorazepam (Ativan), phenobarbital (Donnatal), and zolpidem (Ambien) as their effectiveness will be increased, causing excessive sleepiness.
Magical use: Lemon balm is used in spells to bring animal healing, compassion, endings, fertility, happiness, healing, longevity, love, mental, prosperity, psychic, release, success and youth.
Superstition and folklore: In ancient times lemon balm was planted by the front door to drive away evil spirits.
Personal note: In the eleventh century, Arab physician Avicenna, said that it's *'a wonderful plant for cheering up and comforting the heart'*.

LILAC

Scientific Name(s): *Syringa vulgaris*
Common Name(s): White lilac; purple lilac;

Although rarely used in medicine, lilac was only introduced into Britain in the 16th-century from eastern Europe and the Middle East. Due to their pleasant fragrance, lilacs have become a popular ingredient in perfumes and cosmetics. When used as an essential oil, they have been known to treat skin disorders, combat bacterial and fungal infections, prevent stomach disorders, and act as a fever reducer. In aromatherapy, lilacs can help fight depression and increase relaxation.

Simple: Fill jar with freshly picked flowers with a little room at the top. Pour over clear honey to the top and cap. Allow to infuse for at least 6 weeks. No need to strain afterwards – eat the flowers along with the honey! Great for adding to recipes, spreading on bread, or adding to teas.

Magical use: Lilacs have come to be associated with banishing and getting rid of negative energies – and that may well be due to its strong but delicate fragrance. Plant lilacs around your property to keep out those who might do you harm, or cut some to keep indoors as a way of preventing malevolent spirits, or other ghosts from hanging around.

Superstition and folklore: In certain parts of the country the shrub, especially the white-flowered variety, was reputed to be unlucky. Edwin Radford says in the *Encyclopedia of Superstitions*:

> *The purple and red varieties are usually less feared, but even they are sometimes excluded from house-decorations as bringers of misfortune... An interesting detail about the lilac tradition is that ... it is found only in some English districts, especially in the Midland counties, and is quite unknown elsewhere.*

During the English Civil War, a bowl of lilac in the window showed that the householder had royalist sympathies and, the family would have been unlucky indeed if they'd been betrayed by a simple floral arrangement. My grandmother, who was a staunch monarchist, always had a bowl of lilac in the front window while the shrubs were in bloom in the garden.

Personal note: Lilacs have a deep-rooted history originating in ancient Greek mythology with Pan, god of forests and fields, who was hopelessly in love with a nymph named Syringa. One day he was pursuing her through a forest and, afraid of his advances, she turned herself into a lilac shrub to disguise herself. To Pan's surprise, he could not find Syringa, but he did find the shrub. Because a lilac shrub consists of hollow reeds, he cut the reeds and created the first pan pipe. The scientific name for lilac is *Syringa vulgaris*, and the name is derived from the Greek word *syrinks* which means pipe.

LIME

Scientific Name(s): *Tilia europea*
Common Name(s): Linden;

With their mild, pleasant taste, lime flowers are among the most popular herbal relaxants; they are useful in treating anxiety, migraine and a range of circulatory problems. Linden tea is much used on the Continent, especially in Provence, where stocks of dried lime-flowers are kept in most households for making *tilleul* a light and lively *tisane* of the tree's fragrant flowers and leaves, prized for its subtle floral quality as well as its mild digestive and sleep benefits. The honey from the flowers is regarded as the best flavoured and the most valuable in the world.

Simple: Lime-flowers are used in infusions or made into a distilled water as a household remedy for indigestion. Pour the boiling water over the 1-3 teaspoons of lime flowers. Cover the cup to retain the steam in the drink. Leave to infuse for 10–15 minutes and drink as a tonic. Lime flower or linden blossom has a calming effect and was said to be drunk by WWII soldiers to bring about calmness; whilst doctors during this time used the herb as a tranquiliser. An infusion of lime flowers can help induce sweating, which will lower body temperature.

DANGER: DO NOT take with Lithium as linden can cause the liver to accumulate excessive levels of lithium. Any increase in lithium levels in the body can result in serious side effects.

Magical use: Linden flowers are often used in love and protection spells, and incenses.

Superstition and folklore: The lime tree or linden is important in the mythology, literature, and folklore of a number of cultures.

Personal note: J R R Tolkien composed the poem *Light as Leaf on Lindentree* which was originally published in 1925 in volume 6 of *The Gryphon* magazine. After many emendations it was later included in *The Lord of the Rings* as a song sung by Aragorn about the tale of Beren and Lúthien.

LOVAGE

Scientific Name(s): *Levisticum officinale*
Common Name(s): Sea parsley;

Has a sweet, aromatic taste and is one of the old English herbs much used in cooking. The leaves can be used in salads, or to make soup or to season broths, and the roots can be eaten as a vegetable or grated for use in salads. Its flavor and smell can be described as a mix of celery and parsley, but with a higher intensity of both of those flavors. Lovage is helpful for both colic and flatulence, especially in conjunction with poor appetite; also, as a gargle and mouthwash for treating sore throats and mouth ulcers.

Simple: A hot lovage infusion of 1 oz dried, leaves, stems and flowers in 1 pint of boiling water is good for chills and colds; cover and strain after 15 minutes. Flavour with honey if desired.

Magical use: In medieval times lovage was used in magic spells. For example, a sprig of lovage and a piece of paper with the names of the lovers was tied up with three threads (red, green, white) and buried along the foundation wall where the couple lived. This spell provided permanent love and brought good fortune in love and marriage. Lovage was also believed to protect against bad spirits.

Superstition and folklore: The lovage leaf has been highly valued in the folklore as a magical plant that inspires partners with love and desire. According to the legend, when used in a meal, it will cause sexual and erotic arousal.

Personal note: The name lovage is from 'love-ache', *ache* being a medieval name for parsley.

MARJORAM

Scientific Name(s): *Origanum vulgate*
Common Name(s): Oregano; wild marjoram;

Valued as something of a cure-all, marjoram was prescribed for indigestion, insomnia, earache, loss of appetite, dropsy and a host of other ailments. The leaves and flowers were made into an aromatic tea to stimulate digestion, relieve flatulence, sooth nerves, cure colds and headaches. Dried and powdered, the leaves were used as snuff to clear nasal congestion. A sweet and savoury pot-herb with a wide range of flavouring uses, marjoram was added to salads, soups, sauces, stuffings, stews and meat dishes.

Simple: Boil water and add marjoram leaves; let it steep for 3 minutes or until fragrant. Strain leaves and pour liquid into tea cup, adding honey to taste and serve while still hot.

DANGER: DO NOT take with Lithium as marjoram can cause the liver to accumulate excessive levels of lithium. Any increase in lithium levels in the body can result in serious side effects.

Magical use: To drive off those who would harm your family; to protect home or business from jinxes, place marjoram leaves in each of the rooms and/or place of business, to deflect bad luck.

Superstition and folklore: The herb was used to scent winding sheets, and was planted on graves to ensure that the dead rested in peace.

Personal note: Introduced into England during the Middle Ages, medieval monks grew it in their gardens not only for its usefulness, but for its fragrance and decoration.

MARSHMALLOW

Scientific Name(s): *Althea officinalis*
Common Name(s): Sweet weed; mallards;

An infusion of marshmallow leaves and flowers is useful for treating dry, congested coughs, and makes an excellent gargle and mouthwash for hoarseness, oral thrush and gum abscesses. The dried root powder is a good drawing compound for splinters and boils. Fresh mallow leaves were used as a poultice for wounds, bruises, sprains, inflammations, stings and insect bites.

Simple: 1 oz leaves and flowers per cup infused for 10 minutes will help relieve a dry cough.

DANGER: DO NOT take with Lithium as marshmallow can cause the liver to accumulate excessive levels of lithium. Any increase in lithium levels in the body can result in serious side effects. **CAUTION:** DO NOT take if you are diabetic as marshmallow can increase the effectiveness of diabetic medications. If you are taking any medications while you are taking marshmallow, remember to take it at least one hour *after* taking your medications. This is because marshmallow is a mucilage that can decrease the amount of medicine your body can absorb orally.

Magical use: The flowers are used in *Beltaine* rituals, for garlands and altar decorations. They can also be added to ritual baths, especially for those to encourage and invoke fertility and lust.

Superstition and folklore: From ancient times mallows were also eaten to *reduce* sexual desire, especially as a countermeasure against aphrodisiacs and love-potions.

Personal note: The modern sugary confection known as marshmallow – which contains no herbal extracts – originated from a soothing sweet recipe made from powered root of the plant.

MEADOWSWEET

Scientific Name(s): *Spiraea Ulmaria*

Common Name(s): Meadsweet; dolloff; Queen of the Meadow; bridewort; Lady of the Meadow;

A peculiarity of this plant is that the scent of the leaves is quite different from that of the flowers. The latter possess an almond-like fragrance and it was one of the fragrant herbs used to strew the floors of chambers. In allusion to this use, Gerard writes:

> *The leaves and floures of Meadowsweet farre excelle all other strowing herbs for to decke up houses, to strawe in chambers, halls and banqueting-houses in the summer-time, for the smell thereof makes the heart merrie and joyful and delighteth the senses.*

It is one of the fifty ingredients in a drink called 'Save', mentioned in Chaucer's *Knight's Tale*, in the 14th-century being called 'medwort', or 'meadwort', i.e., the mead or honey-wine herb, and the flowers were often put into wine and beer. Meadowsweet's most famous claim to medicinal success is as a forerunner of aspirin.

Simple: An infusion of 1oz of the dried herb, or a heaped teaspoon of the fresh herb is widely used as an anti-inflammatory for arthritis and rheumatism; add to a pint of water and steeped for 5-15 minutes is the usual preparation taken in wineglassful doses for the relief of minor pains. Sweetened with honey, it forms a very pleasant diet-drink, or beverage both for invalids and ordinary use, although it will get noticeably more bitter with the longer steeping time. Meadowsweet contains salicylates – a substance similar to that in aspirin and an infusion of the herb is anti-inflammatory and promotes sweating.

DANGER: DO NOT take meadowsweet if you are taking the following medications as it may increase their effectiveness, and cause serious complications: Aspirin, Choline Magnesium Trisalicylate (Trilisate), meperidine (Demerol), hydrocodone, morphine, OxyContin, and Salsalate (Disalcid).

Magical use: Meadowsweet is used for love, peace and happiness - all interesting uses in light of its past uses as a strewing herb! The fresh plant is used as an altar decoration for love magic, and the dried herb can be used in various love potions.

Superstition and folklore: Meadowsweet's long history of use by humans as a healing herb and a sweet-smelling plant has ensured a rich repository of fascinating history and folklore exists around the plant.

Personal note: Archaeological digs of prehistoric graves in a Bronze Age cairn at Fan Foe, west Wales have found traces of meadowsweet with the cremated remains of three people.

MINT

Scientific Name(s): Peppermint (*Mentha piperita*); Watermint (*Mentha aquatica*); Spearmint (*Mentha spicata*); Pennyroyal (*Mentha pulegium*)
Common Name(s): See above

Mints are aromatic, almost exclusively perennial herbs but not all mint varieties are used for culinary purposes. Some are better utilized for their aromatic properties or aesthetic appearances while others are normally treated solely as medicinal plants. Mints were used by ancient physicians long before the Bible mentioned that the Pharisees collected their tithes in mint, dill and cumin. Spearmint was probably introduced into England by the Romans.

Simple: Peppermint forms an important part of our lives; from giving our upset stomach some relief to providing our drinks with a refreshing taste and aroma. Its calmative properties can leave us relaxed, release our stress and mental pressure: that's how good and rejuvenating peppermint is. A cup of peppermint tea can help you in ways more than just one, since it helps in aiding weight loss, reduces heartburn, makes our skin glow and induces sleep. There is barely any side effect of peppermint tea; so, we can drink it any time we want to.

Magical use: According to tradition, burning a handful of mint leaves removes diseases and promotes healing. Keeping a bunch of mint at home ensures the household is protected and attracts favorable energy.

Superstition and folklore: Watermint was one of the three most sacred herbs of the Druids: the others being meadowsweet and vervain.

Person note: Known in Greek mythology as the herb of hospitality, one of mint's first known uses in Europe was as a room deodorizer.

MULLEIN

Scientific Name(s): *Verbascum Thapsus*
Common Name(s): Aaron's Rod; hag's taper; great mullein;

Although potentially poisonous, mullein was prescribed for coughs, respiratory disorders, and all inflammatory ailments. Externally it was used to treat burns, wounds, ulcers, skin diseases, haemorrhoids and rheumatic aches and pains. The smoke from the burning leaves was inhaled to relieve asthma; while mullein tea was taken as a sedative and pain-killer.

Simple: Mullein tea is a flavorful beverage that has been used for centuries to treat a variety of ailments, including chronic coughs, colds, and asthma. To make the tea with dried leaves, simply add a small handful of them to a cup of boiling water, then steep them for 15–30 minutes. To prevent throat irritation, use a strainer or cheesecloth to remove as many of the leaves as possible. Or purchase prepackaged mullein tea bags online. The tiny hairs of the plant can also irritate your throat, which is why it's important to strain this tea thoroughly before drinking it even when using tea bags.

Magical use: The name 'hag's taper' refers to the plant's use in the rites, potions and spells of witches.

Superstition and folklore: As a test of fidelity, a lover would bend the stem of a mullein plant in the direction of the lover's house: if the plant died the latter was unfaithful – but if it resumed its upright position then there was no cause for concern.

Personal note: There is some claim that mullein was the mystical herb *moly*, given to Ulysses by Hermes as a protection against the sorcery of Circe.

NASTURTIUM

Scientific Name(s): *Tropaeolum majus*

Common Name(s): Indian Cress; Cress of Peru; Larkes Heel; Yellow Larks Spurr. In 16th-century England it was called 'blood flower of Peru';

Nasturtium plants are best known for their intensely bright yellow, orange, and red flowers, but their lush, round leaves are also edible and incredibly delicious in salads. Both the leaves and petals of the nasturtium plant are packed with nutrition, containing high levels of vitamin C. It has the ability to improve the immune system, tackling sore throats, coughs, and colds, as well as bacterial and fungal infections. Studies have shown that the leaves also have antibiotic properties, and suggest that they are the most effective *prior* to flowering. First imported into Spain in 1569, the English herbalist John Gerard reported having received seeds of the plant from Europe in his 1597 book *Herball, or Generall Historie of Plantes.* Linnaeus's (botanist) daughter, Elizabeth-Christine was the first to notice that on hot summer days at dusk, the stamens and styles at the heart of nasturtium flowers, emit a spark, which scientists say is due to a high content of phosphoric acid.

Simple: Add some nasturtium to your diet today, either in your food, or on it! Or as an infusion for urinary and upper respiratory tract infections pour 1 ltr boiling water over 1 cup of flowers, leaves and buds in a jug. Cover and allow to brew for 15 mins - strain and drink. Can be used as a hair rinse/tonic and as a spray to protect plants against unwanted bugs!

Magical use: Nasturtium flowers will help you invite magic into your life; it restores vitality, warmth and radiates energy by restoring physical energy when under intense mental focus.

Superstition and folklore: Organic gardeners *use nasturtiums* as companion plants in the garden to keep fruits and vegetables susceptible to aphids clear of the pest.

Personal note: The nasturtiums received their common name because they produce an oil similar to that of watercress (*Nasturtium officinale*).

NETTLE

Scientific Name(s): *Urtica dioica*
Common Name(s): Stinging nettle;

Nettles are excellent for regulating bodily functions and are a good cleansing and nutritive herb. A nettle infusion is a good spring cleansing tonic and a help in congestive conditions and water retention. The sting from a nettle can be relieved by rubbing it with a bruised dock-leaf while saying: '*Nettle in, dock out. Dock rub nettle out!'* The sting of a nettle may also be cured by rubbing the part with rosemary, mint or sage leaves. The burning property of the juice is dissipated by heat, enabling the young shoots of the nettle, when boiled, to be eaten as a pot-herb. The spring leaves can be used as a vegetable but by late summer the leaves become a laxative! Its fibre is very similar to that of hemp or flax, and it was used for the same purposes, from making cloth of the finest texture down to the coarsest, such as sailcloth, sacking, cordage, etc.

Simple: Make an inf usion by steeping 1 oz of the herb in a pint of boiling water as a good addition to the diet of anyone recovering from a long illness as a tonic.

CAUTION: DO NOT take nettle if you are diabetic as nettle can increase the effectiveness of diabetic medications. **DO NOT** take with lithium as nettle can cause the liver to accumulate excessive levels of lithium. Any increase in lithium levels in the body can result in serious side effects. **DO NOT** take nettle if you have high blood pressure, or are taking warfarin, or if you are taking sedatives.

Magical use: Folklore worldwide attributes the powers of protection and fertility to this plant. Wisdom handed down from ancient times includes advice on using nettles to protect one's self from lightning; to enhance fertility particularly in men and bestow courage. In Celtic lore, nettles serve as a threshold guardian and nettle fibers have been found in burial cloths from the Bronze Age, also closely linking this plant with the threshold between life and death, and giving credence to the various folklore that describes nettles as growing from or near the dead.

Superstition and folklore: In various parts of Europe, it was believed that the plant was a protection against witches, demons and being struck by lightning.

Personal note: The nettle was one of the nine sacred herbs of the Anglo-Saxons.

OATS

Scientific Name(s): *Avena fatua* (wild) or *Avena sativa* (cultivated)
Common Name(s): Groats;

The oat is a native of Britain in its wild and uncultivated form, and is distinguished by the spikelets of its ears hanging on slender stalks. As it needs less sunshine and solar warmth to ripen the grain than wheat, it furnished the principal grain food of cold northern Europe. Oatmeal in its more popular form for eating is that of porridge, where the ground meal becomes thoroughly soft by boiling, and is improved in taste by the addition of milk and salt. *'The halesome parritch, chief of Scotia's food,'* said Burns, with fervid eloquence, although it was also known for being one of the main constituents of gruel - a thinner version of porridge that may be more often drunk than eaten and may not need to be cooked. Gruel was the staple food of the ancient Greeks, for whom roasted meats were the extraordinary feast that followed sacrifice, even among heroes, while *'in practice bread was a luxury eaten only in towns'*. Roman plebeians 'ate the staple gruel of classical times, supplemented by oil, the humbler vegetables and salt fish', for gruel could be prepared without access to the communal ovens in which bread was baked. In the Middle Ages the peasant could avoid the tithe exacted, usually in kind, for grain ground by the miller of the landowner's mill by roasting the grains to make them digestible, and grinding small portions in a mortar at home. In lieu of cooking the resulting paste on the hearthstone, it could be simmered in a cauldron with water or, luxuriously, with milk.

Simple: Stir up a warm and nourishing bowl of *porridge* for an energizing breakfast. Numerous studies have shown porridge is one of the best choices to start the day for stable and steady weight loss. This is because it is filling, packed with fibre, and can be served in a variety of ways to stop it becoming boring.

Magical use: Money is the primary magical power of oat straw, Perhaps it has to do with the harvests because obviously if the crop was very good, more money was made. It is also excellent in fertility spell work and talismans.

Superstition and folklore: During the Middle Ages, oats were thought to attract vampires, and farmers who grew the grain had garlands of garlic wrapped around their doors and windows.

Personal note: The *Romans* introduced *oats* to other countries in the form of crops which they named 'cereals', after Ceres, the *Roman* goddess of agriculture.

ONION

Scientific Name(s): *Allium cepa*
Common Name(s): Scallion; ramps' wild onion; chives;

Onions are members of the *Allium* genus of flowering plants that also includes garlic, shallots, leeks and chives. These vegetables contain various vitamins, minerals and potent plant compounds that have been shown to promote health in many ways. In fact, the medicinal properties of onions have been recognized since ancient times, when they were used to treat ailments like headaches, heart disease and mouth sores.

Onions were historically used as a preventative medicine during epidemics of cholera and the plague. They were apparently eaten by Roman emperor Nero as a cure for colds, and its reputation has made onions a popular component in the diets of many countries. A 'remedy' that gets passed around every cold and flu season is to place a cut onion in the room of the person who is sick. The claim is that onions have the ability to absorb bacteria and viruses and will actually pull the germs out of the sick person. This is just an old wives' tale and according to the National Onion Association, there is no scientific evidence that a cut raw onion absorbs germs or rids the air of toxins/poisons but this folk remedy to keep raw onions in a sick person's room dates back to the 1500s.

During the bubonic plague, cut onions were placed around homes to keep people from contracting the deadly illness. At the time, it was believed that all illnesses were spread through the air. These clouds of disease - or miasmas - were thought to exist when the air smelled bad. In more recent history, people used the cut onions in the room to protect against the 1918 flu pandemic. In one anecdote, a doctor had his patients place cut onions in their homes and they all stayed healthy while others in the community did not.

Simple: To relieve chilblains – rub half a cut onion dipped in salt on sore chilblains and in no time the itchy, soreness disappears. Apply a slice of raw onion to bee or wasp stings to reduce the irritation, or bind it with a handkerchief or crepe bandage and keep it on for several hours.

Magical use: Use this many-layered food to peel away problems in life and to dispel anger. Wild onions clear away obstacles when peeled to the core.

Superstition and folklore: In medieval times onions were reputed to have the power to ward off snakes and witches, as well as to absorb infection from the plague.

Personal note: A popular and widespread preventative treatment in greyhound racing kennels was to hang a bag of onions from the roof. The onions were cut in half, and changed for fresh ones every couple of days because it was believed they took all the bacteria from the air in the kennel so the dogs were less likely to get any of the air borne kennel coughs, etc.

PARSLEY

Scientific Name(s): *Petroselinum crispum*
Common Name(s): Petersylinge. persely. Persele;
Indigenous to the eastern Mediterranean, parsley has been widely cultivated since the time of the ancient Greeks to the present

day, although there is an old superstition against transplanting parsley plants. The herb is said to have been dedicated to Persephone and to funeral rites by the Greeks and it was afterwards consecrated to St. Peter in his character of successor to Charon. As a herb, just one cup of parsley contains over 1,200 percent of the recommended daily intake of Vitamin K, which is needed for blood clotting, bone health and improvement of calcium absorption in the body, so use generally as a garnish in the kitchen and add sprigs of fresh parsley to salads.

Simple: Parsley infusion is a herbal solution for poor appetite and digestion, and for flatulence and colic. Make parsley tea using fresh or dried leaves: Fresh: ¼ cup of fresh leaves added to 1 cup of boiling water - allow to steep for 5-10 minutes. Dried: Measure out 2 teaspoons of dried parsley leaves. Place the leaves in the bottom of a teacup, pour the boiling water on top, and steep the leaves for 5-10 minutes. Alter the steep time according to personal taste and strain. Parsley tea can seem very bitter, and the flavor becomes stronger the longer it is steeped. Chewing a sprig of parsley is also very effective for reducing garlic breath.

Magical use: Use a small amount of dried herb as an incense with incantations related to physical well-being and happiness, and in rituals for the dead, including communication.

Superstition and folklore: The plant was often associated with the devil, who was reputed to take a large proportion of the sown seeds, thereby accounting for their slow and erratic germination. Indeed, country folk claimed that only the wicked could grow parsley; and those that gave it away, or transplanted it, could expect misfortune.

Personal note: Parsley was held sacred by the Greeks and included in wreathes used to crown victors in the Isthmian Games. Both Greeks and Romans used the herb in funeral rites and to decorate graves.

PEPPERMINT

Scientific Name(s): *Mentha piperila*
Common Name(s): Brandy mint; lammint;

Peppermint is a hybrid of water mint and spearmint, which had been used medicinally in the Old World. There is evidence of peppermint cultivation by the Egyptians, and it is mentioned in 13th-century Icelandic pharmacopeias, although it did not come into general medical use until the 18th-century in England. Commonly used as a remedy for colic, diarrhoea, sluggish digestion, flatulence and the relief of nausea. Prolonged exercise and ill-fitting shoes are common causes of sore feet where the skin can develop painful blisters which may burst and even bleed. A strong infusion of peppermint used as a footbath can help.

Simple: Infuse I teaspoon dried leaves in 1 covered cup of boiling water for 10 minutes. Strain and flavor with honey if required. Drink hot between and after meals to aid digestion.
Magical use: *Peppermint* can be *used* for divination, visualization during lucid dreaming; crush in a paper napkin and inhale the scent; also for purification.
Superstition and folklore: A jar of mint kept in the house freshens the air and keeps flies and mice away. Traditional folk belief holds that a sprig of mint placed in milk will keep it from souring.
Personal note: It is said to aid psychic powers.

PERIWINKLE

Scientific Name(s): *Vinca major*
Common Name(s): Sorcerer's violet; Flower of Death;

The periwinkle was known in Britain by at least Anglo-Saxon times. *Great* for brightening up a shady spot, this ground-hugging, evergreen, trailing groundcover has dark green leaves with yellowish-white edges; Blue flowers appear in spring. As a symbol of immortality, it was traditionally linked with death, and sometimes worn by those about to be executed. The plant is astringent, bitter, detergent, sedative, stomachic and tonic. It contains the alkaloid 'vincamine', which is used by the pharmaceutical industry as a cerebral stimulant and vasodilator. It also contains 'reserpine', which reduces high blood pressure.

Simple: None - as this plant can be poisonous.

CAUTION: DO NOT take periwinkle if you have high blood pressure as it can increase the effectiveness of antihypotensive medicines, causing a sudden, severe drop in blood pressure.

Magical use: An old name, given both in reference to its colour and its use in magic is 'Sorcerer's Violet' (corresponding to its old French name *Violette des sorcier*). It was a favourite flower with 'wise folk' for making charms and love-philtres and was also one of the plants believed to have power to exorcize evil spirits. In Macer's *Herbal* we read of its potency against 'wykked spirytis'.

Superstition and folklore: Hang up on the door in a wreath to protect all within the building.

Personal note: A trailing plant, it was often represented in illuminated designs and engravings.

PLANTAIN

Scientific Name(s): *Plantago spp*

Common Name(s): Ripplegrass; Waybread; Snake-weed; Cuckoo's bread; Soldier's herb; Englishman's foot;

Plantago species have been used since prehistoric times as herbal remedies. Plantain was much used by the Anglo-Saxons as a laxative and for bites and wounds. The herb is an excellent aid for all forms of respiratory congestion – nasal catarrh, bronchitis, sinusitis and middle ear infections – not to mention urinary infections. It also calms the irritation and itching of insect bites, stings and skin irritation is applied directly onto the affected area.

Simple: Infuse 1 cup fresh plantain leaves to two cups of boiling water; cover and let it stand for 5 minutes. For the relief of minor cuts, abrasions stings and scratches bruise fresh, clean leaves and apply to the affected area as a compress.

CAUTION: DO NOT take plantain if you have been prescribed warfarin as it contains high amounts of vitamin K, a clotting agent. This will decrease the effectiveness of warfarin and may result in excess clotting.

Magical use: In spells related to strength, healing, and protection and as a charm against snakebite. It can also be used in any working to enhance the effect of other herbs.

Superstition and folklore: In Serbia, Romania, Bulgaria and Russia, leaves from *Plantago major* are used as a folk remedy to preventing infection of cuts and scratches because of its antiseptic properties.

Personal note: In Old English, *Wegbrade* the *plantago* is one of the nine plants invoked in the pagan Anglo-Saxon *Nine Herbs Charm*, recorded in the 10th century.

POPPY (Field)

Scientific Name(s): *Papaver rhoeas*
Common Name(s): Field poppy; Flanders poppy;

Among the seeds of various species of poppy discovered in an Egyptian tomb dating from 2500BC, were those of the common field poppy. The flowers have long been used as an anodyne for soothing mild aches and pains (e.g., toothache, earache and sore throat), a mild sedative/relaxant, an expectorant for treating catarrh and coughs, as a digestive, and even for reducing the appearance of wrinkles and in making lipstick! Although in

Britain the field poppy is only regarded as a weed, and only a limited amount of the petals are used, it is cultivated in Flanders and several parts of Germany for the sake of its seeds, which are not only used in cakes, but from which an excellent oil is made that is used as a substitute for olive oil. In traditional folk medicine, it was used for gout, aches, and pains. The petals were used to create a syrup that was fed to children to help them sleep.

Simple: None – since it is very slightly narcotic.

CAUTION: DO NOT take poppy if you have been prescribed sedatives or CNS depressants as field poppy has a sedative effect and may increase sleepiness.

Magical use: In the days of antiquity the poppy was valued for its magical properties and throughout the Middle Ages it not only gained popularity due to its medicinal powers but also acquired quite a reputation in connection with folk magic.

Superstition and folklore: In addition to being a symbol of remembrance (the colour of its flowers representing the blood of dead warriors), the poppy has long been associated with fertility.

Personal note: Poppies are companion plants of wheat and barley, and the round-bellied capsules filled with seeds were regarded as a symbol of fertility; it is likely that poppies also played an important role in Demeter's sacred rites at Eleusis.

PRIMROSE

Scientific Name(s): *Primula vulgaris*
Common Name(s) English primrose; first rose; early rose;

A native of Britain and Europe, the primrose – being early flowering – was long considered a herald of spring; its name is derived from the Latin for 'first rose'. The plant is abundant in woods, hedgerows, pastures and on railway embankments throughout Great Britain, and is in full flower during April and May. In sheltered spots in mild winters, it is often found in blossom during the opening days of the year and possesses somewhat similar medicinal properties to those of the cowslip. In the early days of medicine, the primrose was considered an important remedy in muscular rheumatism, paralysis and gout. Pliny speaks of it as almost a panacea for these complaints. An infusion of the flowers was formerly considered excellent against nervous hysterical disorders. *'Primrose tea'* says Gerard, *'drunk in the month of May is famous for curing the phrensie'*. The infusion may be made of 5-10 parts of the petals to 100 of water. *'Of the leaves of Primrose'*, Culpeper tells us, *'is made as fine a salve to heal wound as any I know'*. In ancient cookery the flowers were the chief ingredient in a potage called 'Primrose Potage', while another old dish had rice, almonds, honey, saffron, and ground primrose flowers. [A Plain Plantain]

Simple: see cowslip
Magical use: Primrose flowers have got fairies as their caretakers, and are a symbol of good luck, perfect health, fresh starts etc. The flower is also the symbol of clear spiritually-filled paths ahead and symbolize qualities like purity and honesty.
Superstition and folklore: In folklore it was said that by eating the flowers children could see fairies and although it was lucky to bring thirteen primroses into the house, a single flower would bring misfortune.
Personal note: None of the primula species are closely related to the evening primrose (genus *Oenothera*).

RAGWORT

Scientific Name(s): *Senecio jacobaea*
Common Name(s): Stinking Nanny; St James Wort; ragweed; staggerwort; cankerwort;

Although the plant is unwanted by landowners because of its toxic effect on cattle and horses, and because it is considered a weed by many, it nevertheless provides a great deal of nectar for pollinators. The many names that include the word 'stinking' (and 'Mare's Fart') arise because of the unpleasant smell of the leaves. The Greek physician, Dioscordes recommended the herb, as did the two 'fathers' of herbalism, Gerard and Culpeper. The Oxford ragwort, an introduced species, escaped into the wild from the city's Botanical Gardens in the 19th-century.

Simple: None.

DANGER: DO NOT take ragwort if you are taking the following medications: carbamazepine (Tegretol), phenobarbital, phenytoin (Dilantin), rifampin, or rifabutin (Mycobutin). Ragwort increases the toxic effect of these drugs in the liver and may cause serious complications.

Magical use: According to Cunningham's *Encyclopaedia of Magical Herbs*, *'the Greeks used ragwort as an amulet against charms and spells, and witches were said to ride upon ragwort stalks at midnight in the bad old days of the persecutions'*.

Superstition and folklore: The plant's botanical name is derived from St James the Greater, whose feast day, the 25th July, when it is said to be the time when the plant starts flowering.

Personal note: Ragwort is highly poisonous if eaten by most species of livestock and hay containing ragwort is particularly dangerous.

ROSE

Scientific Name(s): *Rosa canina*
Common Name(s): Dog rose; briar; wild rose;

Rose hip tea is an old folk remedy for colds and mild diarrhoea: it has a delicate, floral flavor that's slightly sweet with a distinct tart aftertaste. Rose petals make a pleasant, soothing and anti-inflammatory infusion; it can also alleviate mild depression and anxiety. Most roses are edible and, in fact, the petals have been used for centuries as a delicate flavoring agent; rose water has also been used to flavor pastry or added to icing or whipped cream.

Simple: Place 1 cup of fresh fragrant rose petals to 3 cups of boiling water and allow to steep for 5 minutes – strain and allow to cool before drinking.

CAUTION: DO NOT take rosehip if you are taking antacids, Estrogen pills, Fluphenazine (Prolixin), Lithium, Warfarin (coumadin), Aspirin, Choline Magnesium Trisalicylate (Trilisate) or Salsalate (Disalcid).

Magical use: It is used to enhance female intuition since it is a flower closely linked to female energy and taking a bath with rose water or a handful of fresh rose petals will help develop this intuition.

Superstition and folklore: The rose is the symbol of secrecy and things spoken of under a rose carved on the ceiling of dining rooms were *sub rosa*, 'under the rose', and therefore in strict confidence.

Personal note: The oldest cultivated rose is thought to be the red *Rosa gallica*, the ancestor of all medieval roses.

ROSEBAY WILLOWHERB

Scientific Name(s): *Epilobium angustifilium*
Common Name(s): Fireweed; Flowering Willow; French Willow; Persian Willow; Rose Bay Willow; Blood Vine; Blooming Sally; Purple Rocket; wickup; wicopy; tame withy;

It is a native of most countries of Europe but in this country, it has apparently become more common than it was in Gerard's day. He tells us he had received some plants of this species from a place in Yorkshire, apparently as a rarity, *'which doe grow in my garden very goodly to behold, for the decking up of houses and gardens'*. It is to be found by moist riversides and in copses, but will sometimes spring up in a town, self-sown, on waste ground recently cleared of buildings: the site of Kingsway and Aldwych in London, adjoining the Strand, where many buildings, centuries old, had been pulled down, was the following summer covered by the rose bay willow-herb, as by a crimson mantle, though no one could explain where the seeds had come from. The same phenomenon was repeated, in Westminster, when other old buildings were demolished for improvements and the ground remained waste for a considerable time.

Rosebay willowherb boasts many beneficial properties and it's regarded as a very useful resource in herbal medicine, especially considering its virtual total lack of side effects. This plant is very effective against mouth infections, **ulcers** and respiratory problems, and those affecting the larynx, the nasal mucosa, the vocal organs and sinuses.

Simple: Being caffeine free, and mildly sedative rosebay willowherb is often brewed in place of regular tea closer to bedtime. Besides its relaxing effect, it is also well known for its anti-inflammatory properties and as an aid to digestion.

Magical use: The herb was considered by Culpeper to be 'anodyne, funereal, melancholic or otherwise Saturnine'.

Superstition and folklore: According to folklore the blooming of the plant indicates the rolling away of the summer, with full bloom marking the beginning of autumn.

Personal note: As the plant often colonized ground that had been cleared by fire, it was commonly known as 'fireweed'.

ROSEMARY

Scientific Name(s): *Rosmarinus officinalis*

Common Name(s): Polar plant; compass-weed; compass plant; *Rosmarinus coronarium*; *Incensier* (Old French);

An old favourite of the Greeks, brought west by the Romans, and used during the Middle Ages as an incense, rosemary has been celebrated in myth, magic and herbal medicines for centuries. We may think of the herb as a delicious flavor enhancer for our meals, but it's much more than that. Traditionally, it was used remembrance and memory and when Shakespeare has Ophelia say: *'There's rosemary, that's for remembrance,'* she is simply giving voice to an age-old belief that the herb actually strengthened the memory if taken internally or hung from the rafters.

Simple: Rosemary infusions are an old herbal remedy for relieving tension headaches; as a stimulant and anti-depressive. Infuse 1 teaspoon dried rosemary tops, leaves or flowers in a covered cup of boiling water for 20 minutes. Strain and flavor with honey to taste. Similar in effect is steeping a handful of chopped fresh springs of rosemary direct from the garden in a bottle of white wine for 3 days. Strain and decant for use.

Magical use: Rosemary is an herb whose correspondences transcend religious boundaries. Know in many vastly different spiritual traditions, this pine-scented culinary herb has been used by witches, Christians, ancient Greeks, and more! Use it to substitute other herbs in spells, or use it for protection, removal of unwanted scenes, and blessings!

Superstition and folklore: *Banckes's Herbal* suggests: *'Make thee a box of the wood of rosemary and smell to it and it shall preserve thy youth'.*

Personal note: Placing a sprig under the pillow at night it was said to ward off evil spirits and bad dreams.

RUE

Scientific |Name(s): *Ruta graveolens*
Common Name(s): Herb of Grace; herbygrass;

A native of southern Europe and the Mediterranean, rue was introduced into England by the Romans, who not only believed that it improved eyesight, but that it had the power to bestow second sight on those who consumed it regularly. The bitter taste of its leaves led to rue being associated with the (etymologically unrelated) verb *rue* 'to regret'; rue is well known for its symbolic meaning of regret and has sometimes been called 'herb-of-grace' in literary works. It is another of the flowers distributed by Ophelia in Shakespeare's *Hamlet*. Pliny said it was one of the Roman's chief medicinal plants, and *'an antidote for all poisons'*. Rue was preferred as a substance to keep away pests and insects away primarily owing to the plant's robust and stale fragrance. Interestingly, during the Middle Ages, whenever the rich went outdoors, they took along with them a small bouquet of the rue flowers to wade off the lice of vagabonds and beggars.

Simple: The tops of fresh rue shoots are gathered before the plant flowers, and are used fresh or dry as a home remedy for coughs and stomach issues such as flatulence. To prepare an infusion with the rue, add one to two teaspoons of the dehydrated herb in a cup of boiling water and leave it to permeate for 10-15 minutes. **CAUTION: DO NOT** take rue if you have been prescribed the following medications as they may increase your sensitivity to sunlight: amitriptyline (Elavil), Ciprofloxacin (Cipro), norfloxacin (Noroxin), lomefloxacin (Maxaquin), ofloxacin (Floxin), levofloxacin (Levaquin), sparfloxacin (Zagam), gatifloxacin (Tequin), moxifloxacin (Avelox), trimethoprim/ sulfamethoxazole (Septra), tetracycline, methoxsalen (8-methoxy-psoralen, 8-MOP, Oxsoralen), and Trioxsalen (Trisoralen).

Magical use: The herb was worn for luck, and as a protection against witchcraft, the evil eye and the plague. It was sacred to the god Pan and features in Dion Fortune's novel, *The Goat-Foor God*.

Superstition and folklore: In medieval times, rue was placed near magistrates to protect them against 'goal fever' brought into court by prisoners.

Personal note: The phrase 'rue the day' comes from the custom of throwing a bunch of rue in the face of one's enemy.

SAGE

Scientific Name(s): *Salvia officinalis*
Common Name(s): Sawge; common sage;

It has been cultivated for culinary and medicinal purposes for many centuries in England, France and Germany, being sufficiently hardy to stand any ordinary winter outside. Gerard mentions it as being in 1597 a well-known herb in English gardens, several varieties growing in his own garden at Holborn. Many kinds of sage have been used as substitutes for tea, the Chinese having been said to prefer sage tea to their own native product, at one time bartering for it with the Dutch and giving thrice the quantity of their choicest tea in exchange.

Simple: A strong infusion of the fresh herb makes an ideal mouthwash and gargle for mouth ulcers, swollen gums and sore throats. Place 1 teaspoon in 1 cup of boiling water; cover and strain after 10 minutes. A cure for sprains: bruise a handful of sage leaves and boil them in a gill of vinegar for 5 minutes; apply this in a folded napkin as hot as it can be borne to the part affected.

DANGER: DO NOT take sage if you are diabetic taking diabetic medications, taking CNS depressants or anticonvulsants as sage interacts with these medications detrimentally.

Magical use: Burn sage incense when seeking knowledge or guidance on a difficult decision. Sage is used to promote wisdom and bring in good luck. It builds emotional strength and may help to heal grief. When crushed, the dried herb is added to purification incenses.

Superstition and folklore: Folklore maintained that when sage flourished in a garden the owner's business would prosper, but when it withered and died their business would fail.

Personal note: Considered sacred by the Greeks and Romans, the latter gathered the herb in a special ceremony that involved the use of a knife not made from iron (because sage reacts with iron salts).

ST JOHN'S WORT

Scientific Name(s): *Hypericum perforatum*
Common Name(s): Common St John's wort; perforate St John's wort;

St John's wort owes its name to the fact that it flowers at the time of the summer solstice around St. John's Day on 24th June. Spartan warriors used its oil to treat their wounds after the battle and was administered as a remedy by the Roman military doctor Proscurides as early as the 1st century AD, although it was mainly used for magic potions during the Middle Ages. Paracelsus was one of the first doctors to concern themselves with St John's wort and the herb is most commonly used for treating 'the blues' - or mild depression and symptoms that sometimes go along with moods such as nervousness, tiredness, poor appetite, and trouble sleeping. Of all the many herbal remedies that have been proven highly effective, St. John's wort is often used for alleviating anxiety, stress, seasonal affective disorder, insomnia and depression. A trick is to pick a flower or bud and squeeze it between your fingertips, if there is a deep red stain, this is the color of hypericin, one of the active constituents of the plant. St John's Wort is an herb that is best used fresh, as air-drying tends to degrade activity.

Simple: Fresh St. John's Wort tea is delicious and has a delightful light lemony flavour. Steep 2-3 teaspoons of fresh flowers in hot water for 4 minutes, and then strain the flowers out.
DANGER: DO NOT take St John's wort if you are taking the following medications as the herb mixed with them can cause

severe or life-threatening complications: Alprazolam (Xanax), Aminolevulinic acid, Amitriptyline (Elavil), Birth control pills, Cyclosporine (Neoral, Sandimmune), Digoxin (Lanoxin), Fenfluramine (Pondimin), Imatinib (Gleevec), Irinotecan (Camptosar), lovastatin (Mevacor), ketoconazole (Nizoral), itraconazole (Sporanox), fexofenadine (Allegra), triazolam (Halcion), fluoxetine (Prozac), paroxetine (Paxil), sertraline (Zoloft), amitriptyline (Elavil), clomipramine (Anafranil), imipramine (Tofranil), nevirapine (Viramune), delavirdine (Rescriptor), efavirenz (Sustiva), amprenavir (Agenerase), nelfinavir (Viracept), ritonavir (Norvir), saquinavir (Fortovase, Invirase), meperidine (Demerol), hydrocodone, morphine, OxyContin, etoposide, paclitaxel, vinblastine, vincristine, vindesine, ketoconazole, itraconazole, amprenavir, indinavir, nelfinavir, saquinavir, cimetidine, ranitidine, diltiazem, verapamil, corticosteroids, erythromycin, cisapride (Propulsid), fexofenadine (Allegra), cyclosporine, loperamide (Imodium), quinidine, amitriptyline (Elavil), Ciprofloxacin (Cipro), norfloxacin (Noroxin), lomefloxacin (Maxaquin), ofloxacin (Floxin), levofloxacin (Levaquin), sparfloxacin (Zagam), gatifloxacin (Tequin), moxifloxacin (Avelox), trimethoprim/ sulfamethoxazole (Septra), tetracycline, methoxsalen (8-methoxypsoralen, 8-MOP, Oxsoralen), and Trioxsalen (Trisoralen), Nefazodone (Serzone), Nortriptyline (Pamelor), Paroxetine (Paxil), Pentazocine (Talw Sertraline (Zoloft) in), Phenobarbital (Luminal), Phenprocoumon, Phenytoin (Dilantin), Reserpine, Barbiturates, Sertraline (Zoloft), Tacrolimus (Prograf, Protopic), Tramadol (Ultram) and warfarin (Coumadin).

Magical use: As a protection against evil, the herb was once known as *Fuga daemonium*, or the 'devil's flight', because its scent was said to be so abhorrent to the devil that he was forced to keep well away.

Superstition and folklore: Superstition claimed that those treading on the plant after sunset would be carried away by a fairy-horse on a wild journey that would last the entire night.

Personal note: Some say the herb takes its name from the Knights of St John, who used it to treat those wounded in the Crusades.

SHEPHERD'S PURSE

Scientific Name(s): *Capsella bursa-pastoris*
Common Name(s): Shepherd's Bag; Shepherd's Scrip; Lady's Purse; Witches' Pouch; Rattle Pouches; Case-weed; Pick-Pocket; Pick-Purse; Poor Man's Parmacettie;

Found world-wide with the exception of the tropics, this plant is one of the most common of weeds that can grow from a single stem in crack in the pavement to a bush on wasteland.

Traditionally, it was used for all forms of internal bleeding and the leaves to staunch bleeding during WWI in the trenches. In more modern times it was used specifically for heavy menstrual bleeding, and can also be used to treat diarrhoea and cystitis.

Simple: In modern herbal medicine the whole plant is employed, dried and administered in infusion made with an ounce of the plant to 12 oz of water, reduced by boiling to ½ pint, strained and taken cold for cystitis.

CAUTION: If you are taking CNS depressants, you should not take shepherd purse as it will cause excessive drowsiness.

Magical use: Magically the plant guides us to balance the energies of opening and contracting since it can turn barren sandy soils into fertile ground again; it offers us the wisdom on how to do this within ourselves It is important to *use* fresh plant for the magical infusion, because the potency is lost if the ingredients are dried.

Superstition and folklore: Eating the seeds of the first three shepherd's purse plants one sees is said to protect against all manner of diseases for the rest of the year.

Personal note: Shepherd's purse was said to be the principal herb in the blue 'Electric Fluid' used by Count Matthei to control hemorrhage. Derived from a combination of *electro* (referring to an electric bio-energy content supposedly extracted from plants and of therapeutic value, rather than electricity in its conventional sense) and *homeopathy* (referring to an alternative medicinal philosophy developed by Samuel Hahnemann in the 18th century) and dismissed as 'utter idiocy' by his peers.

SKULLCAP

Scientific Name(s): *Scutellaria spp*
Common Name(s): Mad-dog weed; hoodwort;

Despite the rather ominous sounding name, skullcap has been used for centuries by herbalists as an effective nerve tonic and sedative. Its common uses include relief of nervous tension, anxiety and nerve pain. Skullcap tea before bed helps to calm all those nagging aches, pains and worries that can interfere with a restful sleep. Today, this plant is widely available in supplement form and purported to provide an array of health benefits, from boosting heart health to relieving anxiety. The common or greater scullcap is fairly common in England, though rare in Scotland and local in Ireland.

Simple: Dried parts of the plant, such as its leaves, are used to brew tea in an infuser. Pour 1½ to 2 cups of boiling water over 1 teaspoon of the herb and allow to steep for 3-4 minutes. Feel free to add a little honey, if desired and enjoy!
Magical use: A small bag of this herb beneath the pillow is excellent for preventing nightmares and as a restorative after a psychic attack; or recovery from exorcism or other magical trials. Also, for trance, psychic workings and oracular dreams.
Superstition and folklore: Due to its gentle relaxing effects, skullcap became a popular treatment in the 1700s for hydrophobia or rabies, resulting in one of its common names, mad-dog weed.
Personal note: It's used by vets to help calm dogs suffering

from excitability, apprehension and phobias such as fear of thunderstorms, fireworks and gunfire. **CAUTION:** Always consult a vet before use.

SORREL

Scientific Name(s): *Rumex acetosa*
Common Name(s): Common sorrel; green sauce; sour leaves; cuckoo meat;

A native of Britain, sorrel has been valued for its culinary and medical properties since ancient times. The name comes from the old French for sour and it was used to cleanse the blood, ease constipation, reduce fever, treat jaundice, and remedy urinary, kidney and liver disorders. As a poultice it was used for infected wounds, boils, ulcers and various skin complaints. In medieval times sorrel was an important vinegar and pot vegetable. The main use of the herb, however, was as an herbal remedy for scurvy, due to the high content of vitamin C in the leaves. An old writer tells us:

> *The apothecaries and herbalists call it Alleluya and Paniscuculi, or Cuckowes meat, because either the Cuckoo feedeth thereon, or by reason when it springeth forth and flowereth the Cuckoo singeth most, at which time also Alleluya was wont to be sung in Churches.*

Simple: Externally, the fresh leaves or decoction made from them were also used as a compress on wounds (especially burns) and for various skin problems such as rashes, inflammations, and pimples.
Magical use: Place in sickrooms to aid in recuperation from illnesses and wounds.
Superstition and folklore: Folklore says that the cuckoo ate the plant to lubricate its vocal cords, hence the name 'cuckoo meat'.
Personal note: The name derives from the Latin 'to suck' – a

reference to the use of the leaves by Roman soldiers to relieve thirst.

SPHAGNUM MOSS

Scientific Name(s): *Sphagnum cymbifolium*
Common Name(s): Bog moss; peat moss;

It is found in wet and boggy spots, preferably on peat soil, mostly near heather, on all our mountains and moors, in patches small or large, usually in water free from lime, the plants growing so close together that it often forms large cushions or clumps. It is seldom found in woods; it grows best on heath moors, in water holes. Towards the end of the WWI, the British Government was using tons of sphagnum moss as surgical dressings, placed directly on to wounds when supplies of cotton bandages could not be met. Fortunately, this folk remedy had not faded from memory and it is still used is rural areas. A Gaelic Chronicle of 1014 relates that the wounded in the battle of Clontarf *'stuffed their wounds with moss'*, and the Highlanders after Flodden stanched their bleeding wounds by filling them with bog moss and soft grass.

Simple: There is a long healing tradition involving natural products like mould, and spiders' webs, lichens and mosses to treat wounds and speed healing. They are usually applied directly to the skin and their proven effectiveness no doubt comes from their natural antibiotic properties.
Magical use: None specific apart for healing.
Superstition and folklore: There are numerous Celtic superstitions about misfortune following those who remove peat (moss) from a location without permission.
Personal note: It is also said that stricken deer have been known to drag their wounded limbs to the moss beds.

STONECROP

Scientific Name(s): *Sedum acre*
Common Name(s): Sedum; wall-pepper;

A native of Britain, stonecrop grew wild on roofs, rocks, walls, sand dunes and dry grassy slopes. It was used to stem bleeding, heal ulcers and sores, treat scurvy and scrofula (the king's evil), resist fevers, expel poisons, treat haemorrhoids and kill intestinal worms. Culpeper wrote that *'the juice take inwardly excites vomiting'*. The older herbalists considered the white stonecrop to possess all the virtues of the houseleek. The leaves and stalks were recommended and used for all kinds of inflammation, being especially applied as a cooling plaster to painful hemorrhoids.

Simple: One of its most well-known uses is as an effective and harmless corn-remover.
Magical use: Incorporate the plant into charms and spells that encourage a peaceful marriage and happy home.
Superstition and folklore: The plant was said to repel witches and protect a house from fire and lightning.
Personal note: Handling can cause blisters and skin irritation.

STRAWBERRY (Wild)

Scientific Name(s): *Fragaria vesca*
Common Name(s): Wood strawberry;

A native of Britain, wild strawberries were known to the ancient Britons, Romans and Anglo-Saxons; evidence from archaeological excavations suggests that *Fragaria vesca* has been consumed by humans since the Stone Age. In medieval healing they were used for wounds, stomach and urinary disorders, dysentery and digestive upsets. Strawberry leaf tea was taken as a tonic after illness, and for anaemia and bad nerves.
Simple: For one person: pick a small handful of green, healthy

leaves. Wash and chop roughly. Place in an infuser in a pot or mug of boiled water for three to five minutes. Remove infuser. Breathe in the fresh green aroma, and enjoy! There is no clinical proof that drinking strawberry tea, specifically, provides any health benefits. There is, however, evidence that compounds in the plant may reduce the risk of cardiovascular diseases.

Magical use: Very useful for any work requiring courage when negotiating precarious relationships - these little strawberries can help 'sweeten' a foe or person, or can be used to encourage them to see you in a clear, truthful light. Wild strawberry's reclusive personality is helpful in matters that require people to make the extra step to see what's really there underneath all the veneer and camouflage. [*Witchcraft 101*]

Superstition and folklore: A symbol of perfection and righteousness, in medieval art and literature it also represented sensuality and earthly desire.

Personal note: Woodland strawberry fruit is strongly flavored, and is still collected and grown for domestic use and on a small scale commercially for the delight of gourmets.

TANSY

Scientific Name(s): *Tanacetum vulgare* or *Chrysanthemum vulgare*
Common Name(s): Gold buttons; garden tansy;

Tansy is native to Eurasia and is found in almost all parts of mainland Europe, as well as Britain and Ireland. Tansy has a long history of use. It was first recorded as being cultivated by the ancient Greeks for medicinal purposes. In the 8th century AD it was grown in the herb gardens of Charlemagne and by Benedictine monks of the Swiss monastery of Saint Gall. Tansy was used to treat intestinal worms, rheumatism, digestive problems, fevers, sores, and to bring out measles. In England tansy is placed on window sills to repel flies; sprigs were placed in bed linen to drive away pests, and it has been used as an ant repellent.

Simple: None. Although tansy tea was prescribed as a general tonic, this plant can be highly toxic and is rarely used by modern herbalists.

CAUTION: DO NOT take Tansy in conjunction with alcohol as it causes sleepiness and drowsiness.

Magical use: Tansy was used to ward off evil and disease. It could be hung above stable doors to protect the animals against evil spells and illness. Planted around the house it drives away thunder and lightning. Incense made from this herb was used to smudge children for protection and cleansing. It was also used as a funerary herb.

Superstition and folklore: The botanical name is derived from the Greek for immortality, or to the ancient use of the plant in embalming or preserving corpses. The leaves, wrapped around meat, were said to act as a preservative and fly repellant.

Personal note: In medieval times tansy was used as a substitute for spices like nutmeg and cinnamon.

THYME

Scientific Name(s): *Thymus vulgaris*
Common Name(s): Garden or wild thyme;

It is cultivated now in most countries with temperate climates, though we do not know at what period it was first introduced into northern countries. It was certainly commonly cultivated in England before the middle of the sixteenth century, and is figured and described by Gerard. Thyme is excellent for infectious or dry coughs, whooping cough and bronchitis. As an antiseptic herb it is a good mouthwash and gargle for sore gums, sore throats and laryngitis. It is also a useful lotion for thrush, athlete's foot, and other fungal infections. As a digestive herb it is helpful for poor appetites and flatulence.

Simple: Place three sprigs of thyme in tea cup and pour over boiling water to cover. Cover cup and allow to steep for 10 minutes. Strain and serve, with honey and/or lemon.

CAUTION: DO NOT take thyme if you have been prescribed anticoagulants or antiplatelet medications as thyme may slow blood clotting and cause excessive bruising and bleeding.

Magical use: Use to fumigate the home or make a room spray with thyme to dispel melancholy, hopelessness and other mellow but negative vibrations, especially after a family tragedy or during a long sickness.

Superstition and folklore: Sleeping on a pillow stuffed with thyme was recommended for giddiness and nightmares.

Personal note: The plant's botanical name *Thymus* is derived from the Greek 'to fumigate' – referring to its use as incense in temples.

TOADFLAX, YELLOW

Scientific Name(s): *Linaria vulgaris*

Common Name(s): Fluellin; Pattens and Clogs; flaxweed; ramsted; snapdragon; churnstaff; dragon-bushes; brideweed; yellow rod; larkspur; Lion's Mouth; Devils' Ribbon; Eggs and Collops; Devil's Head; Pedlar's Basket; gallwort; rabbits; doggies; Calves' Snout; Eggs and Bacon; Buttered Haycocks; Monkey Flower;

A native of Britain, yellow toadflax flourished in the hedges, banks, meadows, waste ground and roadsides. The whole plant was used to make medicine for digestive and urinary tract disorders. It was also used to reduce swelling, relieve water retention by increasing urine production (as a diuretic), and cause sweating. The fresh plant was sometimes applied as a poultice to sooth haemorrhoids, and an ointment of the flowers has been employed for the same purpose. A cooling ointment was also made from the fresh plant - the whole herb being chopped and boiled in lard till crisp, then strained. The result was a fine green ointment, a good application for piles, sores, ulcers and skin eruptions. The juice of the herb, or the distilled water, was considered a good remedy for inflammation of the eyes, and for cleansing ulcerous sores. Among the many old local names given to this plant we find it called 'gallwort', on account of its bitterness, one old writer affirming that it received the name because an infusion of the leaves was used '*against the flowing of the gall in cattell*'. Yellow toadflax has a long history of herbal use. It acts mainly on the liver and was once widely employed as a diuretic in the treatment of oedema, although it is little used now.

Simple: None. The plant should be used with caution and should preferably only be prescribed by a qualified practitioner.

Magical use: At that time, many people also believed that yellow toadflax seeds held a mystic power. Three seeds strung on a linen thread made a charm sufficiently potent to protect one from all evil. And any spell cast upon you could be broken by walking around a yellow toadflax in full bloom three times. [*A History of Herbal Plants*]

Superstition and folklore: Boiled in milk, the plant was said to yield an excellent fly poison, and it is an old country custom in parts of Sweden to infuse toadflax flowers in milk and stand the infusion where flies are troublesome.

Personal note: The flowers are mostly visited by bumblebees.

VALERIAN

Scientific Name(s): *Valeriana officinalis*
Common Name(s): Garden heliotrope; common valerian;

Valerian's old name '*All-heal*' gives an indication of just how much regard this herb was held in the Old World, where it was used since Biblical times as an incense and its name was *'Spikenard'*. The name valerian itself comes from the same origin of the Latin word for *'valere'* meaning to *'be well'*, or *'be strong'*. Similar to the root of the word *'valour'*, for this is a herb that was known to markedly increase a person's strength and courage. In the Middle Ages valerian was widely used to treat epilepsy. The German abbess/herbalist St Hildegard of Bingen wrote warmly on the herb for sleep in the 12th-century. Valerian was also used in the First World War to treat soldiers suffering from shell-shock; likewise, it was prized by Londoners during the Blitz in WWII.

Simple: Valerian calms nervous tension and stress, useful for pre-examination nerves, nervous exhaustion and tension headaches. Traditionally the part to use is the root and bearing in mind the above-ground parts are weaker than the root and that fresh herb is weaker than dried, the leaves and flowers can be used to make a herbal tea. If using the fresh leaves/flowers, use an infuser but don't pour the water while it's still boiling, since that level of heat may actually degrade the active components in valerian tea. Instead, wait a few seconds after the water stops boiling before pouring. Cover the cup and let the tea steep for 5 minutes. If using the root, use 1 teaspoon per cup of hot water. Cover and steep 10-15 minutes.

DANGER: DO NOT take valerian in conjunction with the following medications because serious complications may occur: Alprazolam (Xanax), clonazepam (Klonopin), diazepam (Valium), lorazepam (Ativan), midazolam (Versed), temazepam (Restoril), triazolam (Halcion), pentobarbital (Nembutal), phenobarbital (Luminal), secobarbital (Seconal), thiopental (Pentothal), fentanyl (Duragesic, Sublimaze), morphine, and propofol (Diprivan).

Magical use: Sprinkle valerian at the front door to deter unwanted visitors, or hang the leaves around the home to promote harmony amongst loved ones. Or grow a pot of the herb by the door.

Superstition and folklore: In English folklore, valerian was believed to have aphrodisiac qualities and a young woman who carried a sprig of it was said never to lack ardent lovers!

Personal note: It was also believed to possess the ability to increase psychic perception.

VERVAIN

Scientific Name(s): *Verbena officinalis L.*
Common Name(s): Simpler's joy; verbena;

Vervain was known as a divine herb in ancient Egypt where it was believed to come from the tears of the goddess Isis when she wept over the death of Osiris. While there are well over 250 species of verbena, vervain refers specifically to the types used for medicinal purposes. Vervain is a calming restorative for debilitating conditions, particularly nervous exhaustion and depression. It is antiseptic to wounds and makes an excellent mouthwash for dental and gum disease. *Verbena officinalis*, the common vervain or common verbena, is the type species and native to Europe; the common names of verbena in many Central and Eastern European languages often associate it with iron.

Simple: Vervain/verbena tea can also be made from the flowers and leaves by adding 1 to 2 teaspoons to a pint of boiled water. To get the most from this herbal tea, you should allow it to steep covered for 10 to 15 minutes. To help with sleep trouble, 1 cup about 30 minutes before bed can be helpful. For quick relief from mild headaches make a cold compress from an infusion of vervain and apply to the forehead and back of the neck until the headache clears.

Magical use: Long associated with divine and other supernatural forces, vervain is a wonder herb with a very versatile set of magical uses. It clears stagnant energy and can be used for cleansing and consecrating a sacred/ ritual space and to cleanse the auras of the participants. It can be used to conduct and direct magical energy and intentions and also to open the psychic channels.

Superstition and folklore: Vervain was also one of the most sacred herbs of the Druids, who are said to have gathered it from shady places before sunrise, especially at the time of the rising of Sirius, the Dog Star. They utilised it in divination, consecration, and ritual cleansing of sacred spaces.

Personal note: Both the ancient Egyptians and Chinese thought this herb had 'hidden powers' and it was the herb of prophecy for the magi - the mystic sages of Persia.

VINEGAR

Scientific Name(s): None
Common Name(s): Wine, cider, malt or distilled

Like honey, vinegar is also a plant-based concoction being made from distilled grain alcohol, wine, champagne, beer, cider and more. While vinegar making may be as old as alcoholic brewing, the first documented evidence of making and use was by the Babylonians around 3000BC. They primarily made vinegar from dates, figs, and beer and used it for both culinary and medicinal purposes. Traces of it also have been found in Egyptian urns. The Greeks and Romans frequently used vinegars made from wine; the Spartans had vinegar as a part of their traditional broth *melas zomos*. Since antiquity, folk medicine treatments have also used vinegar, but there is no evidence from clinical research to support the health claims of many of these home remedies. The use of vinegar to fight infections and other acute conditions dates back to Hippocrates, the father of modern medicine, who recommended a vinegar preparation for cleaning ulcerations and for the treatment of sores. *Oxymel*, a popular ancient medicine composed of honey and vinegar, was prescribed for persistent coughs by Hippocrates and his contemporaries, and by physicians up to modern day.

Simple: Apple cider *vinegar* is a popular *home remedy* for sore throats since its antibacterial properties can help kill off the bacteria that could be causing the problem. It is almost like the holy grail of home remedies — for instance, a shot of it is said to help boost energy, control blood sugar, and promote weight loss. In a large mug of warm water, mix 1 tablespoon of apple cider vinegar with 2 tablespoons of honey for a throat tonic. [*Healthline*]
Magical use: According to legend, in France during the Black Plague, four thieves were able to rob houses of plague victims without being infected themselves. When finally caught, the judge offered to grant the men their freedom, on the condition that they revealed how they managed to stay healthy. They claimed that a medicine woman sold them a potion made of garlic soaked in soured red wine (vinegar). Variants of the recipe, subsequently called 'Four Thieves Vinegar', have been passed down for hundreds of years and are a staple of New Orleans *vodun* practices.
Superstition and folklore: It is said that a courtier in Babylonia (c.5000BC) 'discovered' wine, formed from unattended grape juice, leading to the eventual discovery of vinegar and its use as a food preservative.
Personal note: In order to demonstrate her wealth and power, Cleopatra made a bet with the Roman leader Marc Antony that she could spend 10 million sesterces on one meal. The servants placed in front of her a single vessel containing vinegar; she took one earring off, and dropped the pearl in the vinegar, and when it was wasted away, swallowed it.

VIOLET
Scientific Name(s) *Viola odorata*
Common Name(s): Sweet violet;
A native of Europe, North Africa and the Middle East, sweet

violets have been cultivated for their perfume and healing properties for over 2000 years. Traditional uses of this plant were many, also known as 'heartsease', it was said to 'comfort and strengthen the heart' and was often prescribed for emotional upset. Its most famous use was as a cough syrup, with early European recipes describing how cough medicine was made from the blossoms. It was also used as an infant laxative and a sedative. There is a belief that violet flowers can only be smelled once - whilst not strictly true, it has its basis in a quirk of evolution. Ionone, one of the chemicals that makes up the sweet violet's scent, has the power to deaden the smell receptors once it has been sniffed.

Simple: *Sweet violet leaf tea* can be infused in boiling water and made into a delicious herbal drink. Use 1-2 teaspoon of the leaves to 1 cup of boiling water; infuse for 10 minutes and then strain. Acts as a painkiller and an anti-inflammatory, similar to the active ingredient in aspirin, which is helpful in reducing painful inflammation of the joints and effective against rheumatic pain.

Magical use: Violets can be used in a number of magic charms including: love spells, protection magic, and rebirth/resurrection magic.

Superstition and folklore: Folklore says that violets blooming in autumn foretell the arrival of some kind of epidemic in the following year. Violets were blooming in the autumn preceding the onset of Coronavirus.

Personal note: Although there are about nine British violets, most country folk recognized only two: the sweet violet (with scented flowers) and the dog violet (without scent).

YARROW

Scientific Name(s): *Achillea millefolium*

Common Name(s): Nosebleed; soldier's woundwort; staunchwort; Yarrow is an aromatic and hardy perennial plant that can be found all over the globe in the countryside, in meadows and pastures, as well as the edges of highways, and in cities. The plant was thought to be richly endowed with spiritual properties, so it was preserved in temples and treated with special reverence; used as an amulet to protect against negative energy and evil, capable of overcoming the forces of darkness and being a conductor of benevolent powers. When delving deep into the spiritual world, using our powers of divination and psychic vision, yarrow helps heighten our experience, and assists us in seeing more clearly. In folk-magic, a sprig placed beneath the sleeper's pillow would reveal the following:

Thou pretty herb of Venus Tree
Thy true name is Yarrow
Now who my bosom friend must be
Pray tell thou me tomorrow.

Simple: An infusion of yarrow is useful in relieving the symptoms of colds and chills and recovery from infections, as well as for a wide-range of digestive problems. Infusion - use 1-2 teaspoons per cup of boiling water and steep for 5-10 minutes depending on taste.

DANGER: DO NOT take yarrow if you have been prescribed anticoagulant or antiplatelet medications. Yarrow Slows blood clotting and may cause excessive bleeding and bruising. **CAUTION: DO NOT** take with lithium as yarrow can cause the liver to accumulate excessive levels of lithium. Any increase in lithium levels in the body can result in serious side effects. **DO NOT** take with sedatives as doing so may result in excessive sleepiness or drowsiness.

Magical use: Yarrow stalks have long been used for divination purposes from many different cultures. Yarrow tea can also be drunk prior to divination, and to help the mind focus on a specific issue, or avoid distractions. The herbal infusion can be used as a spray for magical cleansing and protection; or as a room spray to aid divination.

Superstition and folklore: The stalks are traditionally used for casting the *I Ching* and the flowers can be added to dream pillows to encourage prophetic dreams. Rubbing your eyelids with yarrow is said to enhance psychic abilities.

Personal note: It is the plant of the warrior par excellence, as it gives strength and power, but also deep love. Its healing value is equally recognized for both physical and spiritual wounds.

~~~~~~~~~~~~~~~~~~~~~~~~~~~~~

Endpiece: If choosing to obtain supplies of herbal cures from your local health shop, do be aware that the same rules apply when mixing herbal preparations with chemical medicines. Many people may prefer to do this, as special care needs to be taken when using *wild* plants for Simples and general domestic plant medicine because most of those herbs traditionally gathered from the countryside are now completely alien to the majority of modern witches and pagans. Those interested in developing the arte of Simpling would be best advised to start with plants purchased from a garden centre, or home-grown from seed, so that they can be clearly labeled and identified.

Most cultivated plants were originally wild, and a large number of 'wild' plants are garden escapees that have repopulated the countryside. But, by and large, a true witches' herbal would have been dominated by plants from the woods and hedgerows, including those of a toxic nature.

In *By Wolfsbane & Mandrake Root: The Shadow World of plants and Their Poisons*, I pointed out that strangely, to our modern way of thinking, poisoning has always been referred to as an 'arte', possibly because its association can be found in the Greek word *pharmakos*, used to refer to herbal remedies, spell-potions and poisons – and those who crafted them. The association with witchcraft was also echoed in Charles G Leland's inflammatory translation of *Aradia, or the Gospel of the Witches* (1899) with the words ...

And thou shalt be the first of witches known;
And thou shalt be the first of all in the world:
And thou shalt teach the art of poisoning,
Of poisoning those who are great Lords of all;
Yea, thou shalt make them die in their palaces ...

Daniel A Schulke's now highly collectable *Veneficium: Magic, Witchcraft and the Poison Path* offers a valuable insight into this intersection of magic and poison that originated in remotest antiquity and reaches into the present day. In all honesty, witch-lore *is* closely tied to a knowledge of poisonous plants as part of its folk-medicine, simply because it is necessary to know what can kill or cure (in either large or small doses) as part of the oral training; and a wide familiarity with *all* wild plants is an essential skill within traditional witchcraft. Some plants have beneficial components while others can be lethal if the wrong treatment is given. As it's suggested in *Veneficium,* poisonous plants can be utilised as powerful magical ingredients in Circle whenever necessary ... **but not in the Simpler's practice.**

DISCLAIMER: Please be aware that this information is provided solely for informational purposes only. It is neither intended nor implied to be a substitute for professional medical advice. Always seek the advice of your physician or other qualified health provider prior to using any herbs or treatments made from herbs. Do not use any herbal remedies during pregnancy.

Chapter Four

Complains & Ailments

Simples were used to treat common complaints and ailments within the family and not as a substitute for professional medical advice. They were part of cunning-lore and comprised of traditional knowledge that developed over generations within various societies before the era of modern medicine. These home remedies (sometimes also referred to as 'granny cures') may or may not have medicinal properties that treat or cure the ailment in question, as they are typically passed along by laypersons - one of the most popular examples being the highly effective use of chicken soup to treat respiratory infections such as a cold or mild flu.

Try experimenting with herbs singly at first, noting the effect that each one has (or doesn't have) because not everyone reacts to a particular herb in the same way, and build up your collection as you go along and record them in your Journal. These remedies are made from the use of a single plant (not compounds) and here are a few common complaints and ailments that can be treated with Simples and cross-referenced with those listed in the main text.

Air freshener: Agrimony;
Anaemia: Carrot;
Appetite: Angelica; centaury; lovage; parsley; St John's wort; thyme;
Arthritis: Meadowsweet;
Asthma: Coltsfoot; mullein;

Banishing: Angelica;

Boils: Chickweed; marshmallow:
Blood disorders: Angelica; barley; beet; hawthorn; burdock; daisy; gooseberry; vinegar;
Bruises: Betony; plantain;
Burns: Calendula; chamomile: witch hazel: dock; figwort; houseleek; sorrel;

Chilblains: Onion;
Cholesterol: Barley; dandelion; flax;
Colds: Borage: broom; carrot; coltsfoot; elder; garlic; honey; lady's mantle; lemon; lime; lovage; marjoram; meadowsweet; yarrow;
Constipation: Briar; flax;
Corns: Stonecrop;
Coughs: Coltsfoot; daisy; horehound; hyssop; marshmallow; mullein; nasturtium; rue;
Cuts and Abrasions: Betony; blackberry; calendula; cinquefoil; ivy; lady's mantle; plantain;
Cystitis: Shepherd's purse;

Depression: Borage; heather; rosemary; St John's wort;
Detox: Barley; briar; broom; burdock; heather;
Diarrhoea: Blackberry; briar; gorse; herb Robert; peppermint; shepherd's purse;
Digestion: Apples; angelica; anise; barley; beet; briar; carrot; centaury; chamomile; dandelion; dill; fennel; honeysuckle; lemonbalm; lime; lovage; marjoram; mint; parsley; peppermint; rosebay willowherb; rosemary; thyme; yarrow;
Divination: Anise;

Eye Wash: Chervil; clover; cornflower;

Fevers: Borage: houseleek; honey; lemon; lime: meadowsweet:
Fractures: Comfrey;

Flatulence: Angelica; lovage; marjoram; parsley; peppermint; rue; thyme;
Footbath: Peppermint;

Gargle: Agrimony; calendula; cinquefoil; elder; herb bennet; herb Robert; lemon; lovage; sage; vervain;

Haemorrhoids: Chervil;
Headaches: Chamomile; cowslip; feverfew; houseleek; lavender; marjoram; meadowsweet; rosemary; valerian;
Healing; Angelica;
Health Charm: Anemone:
Heart: Hawthorn; skullcap;
Heartburn: Centaury; mint;

Insect bites and stings: Basil; calendula; betony; chickweed; houseleek; onion; plantain;
Insect repellent: Basil; tansy;
Insomnia: Agrimony: lavender: chamomile; cowslip; heather; lavender; lemon balm; St John's wort; skullcap; vervain;

Luck: Acorn; cabbage;

Morning sickness: Apple;
Mouth problems: Agrimony; calendula; cinquefoil; lovage; marshmallow; rosebay willowherb;
Mouth wash: Blackthorn; calendula; elder; herb bennet; herb Robert; lovage; parsley; sage; vervain;

Nausea: Apple: chamomile; peppermint;
Negative energy: Acorn; angelica; bay;
Nettle stings: Dock;

Protection: Anemone; angelica; bay; blackthorn; broom;

chamomile; chervil; garlic;

Rashes: Blackberry;
Relaxation: Clove pink; heather; hyssop; lemonbalm; marjoram; mint; rose; rosebay willowherb; strawberry (wild); violet (sweet);
Rheumatism: Meadowsweet; violet (sweet);
Romance: Apple;
Room Spray: Bay; borage; hounds-tongue; lavender; yarrow;

Scalds: Calendula; dock;
Skin disorders: Barley; betony; cabbage; calendula; chamomile; chickweed; cleavers; comfrey; cornflower; dock; gooseberry; groundsel; guelder rose; houseleek; ivy; sorrel;
Sleep aid: Agrimony: lavender; chamomile; rosebay willowherb; St John's wort; vervain;
Sore throat: Agrimony; calendula, blackberry; blackthorn; burdock; herb bennet; honey; lovage; sage; vinegar;
Splinters: Cabbage; marshmallow;
Sprain: Comfrey; sage;
Stress: Borage; valerian;
Swelling: Beech; betony; cabbage; chervil; daisy; figwort;

Tension: Chamomile; clove pink; guilder rose; hyssop; St John's wort; skullcap; valerian;
Tiredness: Centaury;
Tonic: Basil; betony; clove pink; clover; lemonbalm; nettle; strawberry (wild); vinegar; yarrow;

Urinary problems: Barley; betony; briar;

Warts: Broad bean;
Wounds: Blackberry; cinquefoil; comfrey; horsetail; sorrel; sphagnum moss;

Weight loss: Barley; cabbage; lemon; mint; oats; vinegar;

It is impractical to attempt to grow or obtain all of the above, since Simples were opportunistic 'home' remedies – knowing what single plant to use to treat common ailments, with what was to hand and in season. Last year's herbs should be discarded when this year's harvest is complete and shows why we need to maintain a sustainable plant base to get the best out of their magical and medicinal properties.

Endpiece: There has never been a greater demand for natural remedies but it is important to differentiate between conditions that are acute and potentially life-threatening - and minor ailments. When we are ill, it is important to obtain a professional diagnosis and this is particularly important since the former are likely to require conventional treatment, and natural remedies may be ineffective or inappropriate.

Simples come under the heading of domestic plant medicine, or 'folk-medicine' and as Paul Huson points out in *Mastering Herbalism*, that *'if herbalism does have any claim to superiority over regular medicine – and the controversy still rages – it lies in the differences between organically derived drugs and chemically derived ones'*. Nevertheless, if any symptoms persist, we should consult a professional and not delude ourselves that self-diagnosis and herbal treatment will affect a cure.

For the majority of us who are in good health, those minor ailments such as coughs, colds, sore throats, stomach upsets and skin rashes *may* well respond to grandma's remedies, but as *Natural Remedies* tells us, the main danger in using natural remedies at home is the risk that an individual may wrongly diagnose the condition that he or she is suffering from ...

Sometimes the symptoms that appear to have an obvious cause can be misleading. For example, a backache can be a simple cause of muscle strain but there are rare cases when a tumour is responsible. It can also be easy to dismiss symptoms as mild when they may be signs of a serious or deep-rooted problem. For example, an individual may decide that a chronic cough is troublesome, but not really worthy of professional attention. In fact, doctors would argue that persistent coughs always merit medical investigation.

Treating medical conditions at home with natural remedies without receiving a professional diagnosis first is potentially dangerous. Symptoms will be given time to develop and the home treatment you have selected may occasionally exacerbate or disguise an illness. If in doubt, always consult a doctor or a practitioner of complementary medicine, especially if you have been treating yourself at home and have seen no improvement.

In fact, not all of these impromptu cures were herb-based as we discovered in *The Secret People*. When we were kids, our grandmother used to treat us with items from the kitchen shelf for minor ailments. They mostly cured us of the common ailments like stomach upset, burning urination, bee stings, cough and colds. They were very simple and they worked. Like vinegar, bicarbonate of soda, salt and whisky!

Chapter Five

Potpourri

Some of these books are old favourites that stand the test of time, since I return to them time and time again because the advice given in the text is ageless. Unfortunately, many of the on-line herbals are merely repeating information without analysing or comprehending it – or worse still, not accrediting the original authors whereby authentic source material is lost. For most writer's source material provides the original, authoritative, or basic information utilized in research, such as diaries, letters or manuscripts rather than relying on the same old, same old ... These are straight off my own bookshelf as recommended reading:

Healing Power of Celtic Plants by Dr Angela Paine [Moon Books] The idea for this book grew out of the author's life on the borders of Wales, where she lived for a few years. Coming from an academic background in London and spending her time researching the chemistry of medicinal plants, she found herself living, deep in the countryside surrounded by plants that had been used as medicine for centuries, plants native to Britain, plants with a history. This magical place with its sacred wells and standing stones was steeped in Celtic mythology. She was drawn in, absorbed and seduced by ancient traditions kept alive by poets and story-tellers and began to grow the native medicinal plants. Gradually her garden was transformed into a flourishing herb garden, terraced on many levels; her enormous kitchen began to resemble a witch's kitchen, with nettles hanging fan-shaped from the ceiling, racks of drying flowers, jars of tinctures, bottles of *Hypericum* flowers in oil, turning red in the sunshine, shelves filled with ointments, jars of dried herbs, berries and barks … Here we follow in the practical footsteps of the famous Physicians of Myddfai and discover just how much of their knowledge is still applicable today.

Herbal Simples by William Thomas Fernie [Independent] is still recognised as being one of the best and most comprehensive herbal healing reference books ever written. Fernie was a late 19th century medical doctor who possessed endless curiosity, a sharp eye, and an excellent ability to summarize what he had discovered. Not only was he familiar with the great British herbals but he had a healthy respect for folk healing traditions. The result is this remarkable book, which contains endlessly fascinating information about the medicinal powers of plants, and which later herbal writers have mined unmercifully, usually without giving Fernie the credit for which he is due.

The Kitchen & Garden Book of Herb: Knowing, Growing & Cooking by Jessica Houdret and Joanna Farrow [Hermes Books] is more than a mere domestic compendium because it is packed with vital information from designing a herb bed, to harvesting, storing and preserving herbs for use in the home – together with their medicinal uses and culinary recipes. Beautifully photographed, my copy was picked up for £1 in a charity shop, and hovers between kitchen and office, providing a lot of dip-in reading on numerous different levels.

Mastering Herbalism by Paul Huson [Abacus] is a companion title to *Mastering Witchcraft* and really does tell you everything you always wanted to know about the secret power of herbs in practical, step-by-step detail. Published in 1974 this book is still in print and is indispensable for the amateur and professional herbalist alike, not to mention those of a witchcraft persuasion who will find it a valuable, no-nonsense addition to their Craft library. While still a student at the Slade, Huson studied the Qabalah and the Western Esoteric Tradition with Dion Fortune's Society of the Inner Light. In 1964 he worked as Karlis Osis' research assistant at the American Society for Psychical Research in New York; and in 1965 he studied the history and practices of the Hermetic Order of the Golden Dawn and the Stella Matutina under the aegis of Israel Regardie. He subsequently wrote a number of popular books on the occult and allied subjects including the influential *Mastering Witchcraft* (1970); a study of tarot symbolism *The Devil's Picturebook (1971); Mastering Herbalism* (1974); and a second work on tarot symbolism and the history of tarot reading, *Mystical Origins of the Tarot* (2004).

Memory, Wisdom & Healing; The History of Domestic Plant Medicine [Sutton] by Gabrielle Hatfield has gathered material from manuscripts, letters, diaries and personal interviews to produce a detailed picture of the use of domestic remedies in Britain from 1700 to the 21st century. For anyone interested in the factual history of domestic plant medicine and its survival this is still the best book on the market, especially when used as a companion title to *Hatfield's Herbal*. Gabrielle Hatfield is a distinguished historian of plant medicine, having studied botany at Cambridge; took a Ph. D at Edinburgh in plant medicine and is currently a research associate at Kew.

A Modern Herbal by Maud Grieve is another book that has been shamelessly plagiarized over the years without always being accredited. At the outbreak of the First World War, she turned her nursery into a herb farm to address the shortage of supplies of vital medicinal plants. She was a founder member of the short-lived National Herb Growing Association and later president of The British Guild of Herb Growers. During the war she also started The Whins Medicinal and Commercial Herb School. After the war she continued her work promoting the benefits of herbs, writing over three hundred pamphlets or monographs on individual plants. These were edited by Hilda Leyel and were the main source of information in what has become Maud's legacy *A Modern Herbal* which was published 1931.

RHS Encyclopaedia of Herbs & Their Uses by Deni Brown [D&K] who has been a gardener and botanist all her life. After a varied career in horticulture – running an organic smallholding, growing orchids, and working as a herb grower for a nursery (during which time she also trained as a medical herbalist) – she became a freelance botanical writer and has contributed many articles on herbs to a wide range of scientific, herbal and organic gardening magazines. This is the most authoritative illustrated encyclopaedia of herbs yet produced, while the extensive catalogue of colour photographs provides an identification guide for gardener and herbalist alike. The Royal Horticultural Society, through its close links with its membership and it various contacts throughout horticulture, recognised the large and growing demand for a definitive illustrated book on the subject. The Society ranked this demand highly enough to endorse Deni Brown's *Encyclopaedia* and recommend the comprehensive work of reference for the quality, scope and depth of the information in its pages.

It should be obvious, that apart from a single domestic compendium, all the authors of the above titles are authorities in their chosen fields of expertise, which is why, of course, they've been chosen as recommended reading. Needless to say, I do have a reprint of Culpeper's *The English Physitian* (1652), later entitled *The Complete Herbal,* simply because for more than 360 years, his historic guide to herbal remedies had been *the* definitive book on the subject.

Nicholas Culpeper had attempted to make medical treatments more accessible to lay people by educating them about maintaining their health. Ultimately his ambition was to reform the system of medicine by questioning traditional methods and knowledge, and exploring new solutions for ill health. His system was a key development in the evolution of modern pharmaceuticals, most of which originally had herbal origins. Culpeper was a radical in his time, angering his fellow physicians by condemning their greed, unwillingness to stray from Galen and their use of harmful practices such as toxic remedies and bloodletting. The Society of Apothecaries were similarly incensed by the fact that he suggested cheap herbal remedies as opposed to their expensive concoctions!

Nevertheless, as Graeme Tobyn demonstrated in his *Culpeper's Medicine: A Practice of Western Holistic Medicine,* Culpeper's own firm beliefs in astrology and the doctrine of signatures probably contributed to him being imprisoned and tried for witchcraft in 1692. It may well be that the opposition of his practice by high-ranking apothecaries, or perhaps by members of the Royal College of Physicians, became so fierce that this was engineered by false accusations. The offence of witchcraft (or, more correctly, heresy) carried the death-sentence but Culpeper was found not guilty and acquitted of the charge. [cited in *Witchcraft & Demonianism* (1933): C L Ewen *'Nicholas Culpeper of St Leonard's, Shoreditch, Gentleman at St L., on 17yh December, 18 chas. I I, bewitched Sarah Lynge, widow, who languished until 12th January following. Not guilty.'* Sarah Lynge recovered.].

But as Gabrielle Hatfield points out, the 18th-century became a watershed in medicine: official medical practitioners wanted to distance themselves from the earlier, unscientific practice of herbalism. They also wished to appear to have something different and exclusive to offer that was far removed from the 'Simples' of the common people, while the almost exclusive use of Latin in prescriptions and books widened the gulf between the learned and the unlearned. Simple plant remedies were used less and less in official medicine and by the 19th-century, the divorce between herbal medicine and orthodoxy was almost complete.' [Hatfield's Herbal]

Domestic plant medicine has always been an oral tradition because there was never any need for it to be written down, except when it bridged the gap between stable yard and still-room in the country houses.

The last generation of country people who have actual experience of using such remedies is now very elderly and, in most cases, their knowledge has not been written down nor has it been passed on to a younger generation. The reasons for this are various. It is very striking at many elderly country people disclaim all knowledge of 'herbal remedies' but, if asked what their grandmothers did for them when they were ill, will often tell of plant remedies that they regarded just as part of ordinary life – things that 'everybody knew'. Alas, this is no longer common knowledge and it is of urgent importance that the remaining body of knowledge of folk medicine is not lost. [Memory, Wisdom & Healing; The History of Domestic Plant Medicine]

My grandmother died just a couple of months short of her 100th birthday but those remedies *she* used, I still use today and have tried to preserve them in my various books on witchcraft. When I committed my memories to paper in *The Secret People*, I was accused of romanticism, even though my childhood came at the tail-end of this 'extinction'. The current pandemic has offered an opportunity to resurrect some of these old cures because 'cocooning' prevented any trips to the pharmacy; and I've been able to share them with friends and colleagues who found themselves suffering from minor domestic ailments at this time.

For those who would like to help keep these Simples alive, I would say start by familiarizing yourself with the medicinal/healing properties of the 'Scarborough Four' – *parsley, sage, rosemary and thyme* – and develop an intimate relationship with these four popular pot herbs not just in the kitchen, but in day-to-day living, too. Chew parsley for 'garlic-breath' and in a tea to aid digestion; a strong infusion of the fresh sage makes an ideal mouthwash and gargle for sore throats and as a compress for a sprain; rosemary infusions relieve tension headaches and mild depression; while as a digestive herb thyme is helpful for poor appetite and flatulence. Share these Simple remedies with friends and family and this old tradition will start to live again ... Give the herbs as a gift and, who knows, they may form the basis of a Simples herb bed!

Endpiece: In the light of the coronavirus pandemic and the various off-the-wall cures and preventions that crept onto social media, it's reassuring to know that history is merely repeating itself as this recipe for 'plague water' will show.

Plague Water was a name given to a variety of medicinal waters of supposed efficacy against the plague. Most commonly it was a distillation of various herbs and roots that were believed to be efficacious. The recipe given by Eliza Smith was typical in that it contained no less than twenty-two herbal products, both leaves and roots, all steeped in white wine and brandy and then distilled. Samuel Pepys was given a bottle of plague water during the outbreak of the plague in London in 1665 [*Diaries*, Pepys]. OED earliest date of use: 1665

To make Plague-water

PERIOD: England, 17th century | SOURCE: The Closet Of the Eminently Learned Sir Kenelme Digby Kt. Opened, 1677 | CLASS: Authentic DESCRIPTION: A cordial made with white wine & herbs

Take a pound of Rue, of Rosemary, Sage, Sorrel, Celandine, Mugwort, of the tops of red Brambles, of Pimpernel, Wild-draggons, Arimony, Balm, Angelica, of each a pound. Put these Compounds in a pot, fill it with White-wine above the herbs, so let it stand four days. Then still it for your use in a Limbeck [a **distillatory vessel**]

xxxxxxxxx

Taken from *A Boke of Gode Cookery* - 17th Century English Recipes

Sources & Bibliography

Brother Cadfael's Herb Garden, Talbot and Robin Whiteman (Little, Brown)

Culpeper's Medicine, Graeme Tobyn (Element)

Flora Britannica, Richard Mabey (Chatto & Windus)

The Folklore of Plants, T F Thiselton-Dyer (Jefferson)

Green Magic, Lesley Gordon (Webb & Bower)

Green Pharmacy, Barbara Griggs (Norman & Hobhouse)

Hatfield's Herbal, Gabrielle Hatfield (Allen Lane)

Healing Power of Celtic Plants, Dr Angela Paine

Herbal Simples, William Thomas Fernie (Amazon)

The Kitchen & Garden Book of Herbs, Jessica Houdret and Joanna Farrow (Hermes Books)

Mastering Herbalism, Paul Huson (Abacus)

Memory, Wisdom & Healing; The History of Domestic Plant Medicine by Gabrielle Hatfield (Sutton)

A Modern Herbal, Maud Grieve (Courier)

Natural Remedies, Denis Kennedy (Reader's Digest)

Nature's Medicine Chest, Christopher Hedley (Reader's Digest)

The Secret People: Parish-pump witchcraft, Wise-women and Cunning Ways

The RHS Encyclopaedia of Herbs & Their Uses, Deni Brown (DK)

The RHS Really Small Gardens, Jill Billington (Quadrille)

Word-Lore: The Craft of Witches, Melusine Draco (Ignotus)

Other Moon Books by Melusine Draco

Traditional Witchcraft for Urban Living (2012)

Traditional Witchcraft for the Seashore (2012)

Traditional Witchcraft for the Fields & Hedgerows (2012)

Traditional Witchcraft for the Woods & Forests (2012)

The Dictionary of Magic & Mystery (2012)

Magic Crystals, Sacred Stones (2012)

The Atum-Re Revival (2013)

Black Horse, White Horse (2013)

Aubrey's Dog (2013)

By Spellbook and Candle: Cursing, Hexing, Bottling& Binding (2013)

The Coarse Witchcraft Trilogy ed (2013)

Traditional Witchcraft and the Pagan Revival (2013)

Traditional Witchcraft and the Path to the Mysteries (2014)

The Secret People: Parish-pump witchcraft, Wise-women and Cunning Ways (2016)

Pan: Dark Lord of the Forest and Horned God of the Witches (2016)

By Wolfsbane and Mandrake Root: The Shadow World of Plants and Their Poisons (2017)

Having A Cool Yule: How to Survive (and Enjoy) the Mid-Winter Festival (2017)

Divination: By Rod, Birds & Fingers (2018)

The Power of the Elements (2018)

Western Animism: Zen and the Art of Practical Paganism (2018)

Seeking the Primal Goddess (2019)

The Arte of Darkness: Magic and Mystery from the Shadows (2019)

The (Inner-City) Path: A Pagan Approach to Well-Being & Awareness (2020)

Sacred Landscape: Caves & Mountains (2020)

Sexual Dynamics in the Circle (2021)

Moon Books Anthologies

Witchcraft Today – 60 Years On (2014) Moon Books
 'Traditional British Witchcraft'
iPagan Witchcraft (2017) Moon Books
 'Faith & Belief in Traditional British Old Craft'
Seven Ages of the Goddess (2018) Moon Books
 'Beyond the Veil – The Goddess in Witchcraft'
What is Modern Witchcraft? (2018) Moon Books
 'Old Craft for a New Generation'
Ancestral Healing (2020) Moon Books
 'SCHISM & SPLIT: Wounds that can never heal'
Me-Pagan (2021) Moon Books
 'A Time-Capsule of Fun' (*Coarse Witchcraft Trilogy*)
Naming the God (2022) Moon Books
 'Bran'

MOON
BOOKS

PAGANISM & SHAMANISM

What is Paganism? A religion, a spirituality, an alternative belief system, nature worship? You can find support for all these definitions (and many more) in dictionaries, encyclopaedias, and text books of religion, but subscribe to any one and the truth will evade you. Above all Paganism is a creative pursuit, an encounter with reality, an exploration of meaning and an expression of the soul. Druids, Heathens, Wiccans and others, all contribute their insights and literary riches to the Pagan tradition. Moon Books invites you to begin or to deepen your own encounter, right here, right now.

If you have enjoyed this book, why not tell other readers by posting a review on your preferred book site.

Recent bestsellers from Moon Books are:

Journey to the Dark Goddess
How to Return to Your Soul
Jane Meredith
Discover the powerful secrets of the Dark Goddess and
transform your depression, grief and pain into healing
and integration.
Paperback: 978-1-84694-677-6 ebook: 978-1-78099-223-5

Shamanic Reiki
Expanded Ways of Working with Universal Life Force Energy
Llyn Roberts, Robert Levy
Shamanism and Reiki are each powerful ways of healing; together,
their power multiplies. *Shamanic Reiki* introduces techniques to
help healers and Reiki practitioners tap ancient healing wisdom.
Paperback: 978-1-84694-037-8 ebook: 978-1-84694-650-9

Pagan Portals – The Awen Alone
Walking the Path of the Solitary Druid
Joanna van der Hoeven
An introductory guide for the solitary Druid, *The Awen Alone* will
accompany you as you explore, and seek out your own place
within the natural world.
Paperback: 978-1-78279-547-6 ebook: 978-1-78279-546-9

A Kitchen Witch's World of Magical Herbs & Plants
Rachel Patterson
A journey into the magical world of herbs and plants, filled with
magical uses, folklore, history and practical magic. By popular
writer, blogger and kitchen witch, Tansy Firedragon.
Paperback: 978-1-78279-621-3 ebook: 978-1-78279-620-6

Medicine for the Soul
The Complete Book of Shamanic Healing
Ross Heaven
All you will ever need to know about shamanic healing and how to
become your own shaman...
Paperback: 978-1-78099-419-2 ebook: 978-1-78099-420-8

Shaman Pathways – The Druid Shaman
Exploring the Celtic Otherworld
Danu Forest
A practical guide to Celtic shamanism with exercises and
techniques as well as traditional lore for exploring the Celtic
Otherworld.
Paperback: 978-1-78099-615-8 ebook: 978-1-78099-616-5

Traditional Witchcraft for the Woods and Forests
A Witch's Guide to the Woodland with Guided Meditations and
Pathworking
Mélusine Draco
A Witch's guide to walking alone in the woods, with guided
meditations and pathworking.
Paperback: 978-1-84694-803-9 ebook: 978-1-84694-804-6

Wild Earth, Wild Soul
A Manual for an Ecstatic Culture
Bill Pfeiffer
Imagine a nature-based culture so alive and so connected,
spreading like wildfire. This book is the first flame...
Paperback: 978-1-78099-187-0 ebook: 978-1-78099-188-7

Naming the Goddess
Trevor Greenfield
Naming the Goddess is written by over eighty adherents and
scholars of Goddess and Goddess Spirituality.
Paperback: 978-1-78279-476-9 ebook: 978-1-78279-475-2

Shapeshifting into Higher Consciousness
Heal and Transform Yourself and Our World with Ancient
Shamanic and Modern Methods
Llyn Roberts
Ancient and modern methods that you can use every day to
transform yourself and make a positive difference in the world.
Paperback: 978-1-84694-843-5 ebook: 978-1-84694-844-2

Readers of ebooks can buy or view any of these bestsellers by
clicking on the live link in the title. Most titles are published in
paperback and as an ebook. Paperbacks are available in traditional
bookshops. Both print and ebook formats are available online.

Find more titles and sign up to our readers' newsletter at
http://www.johnhuntpublishing.com/paganism
Follow us on Facebook at https://www.facebook.com/MoonBooks
and Twitter at https://twitter.com/MoonBooksJHP